Your Future Begins Today

To my dear Friend
"Virginia Willis"
a true Picture of
Grace & Charm —
Love you,
Jim
7. 11 - 21

Your Future Begins Today

Jim Davidson

Strategic Book Publishing and Rights Co.

Strategic Book Publishing and Rights Co., LLC
USA | Singapore
www.sbpra.net

For information about special discounts for bulk purchases, please contact Strategic Book Publishing and Rights Co. Special Sales, at bookorder@sbpra.net.

ISBN: 978-1-68235-323-3

Book Design: Suzanne Kelly

The COVID–19 Pandemic

Since early 2020, the COVID-19 Pandemic has been like a black cloud that has overshadowed the whole world. To say that we, in the United States of America, "were not prepared" could be the greatest understatement ever made. It has taken the lives of many thousands of our fellow citizens, but Americans have always been resilient and able to bounce back.

While writing a book during a Pandemic is a new experience for me, I just wanted to take a moment here at the beginning to express my deepest condolences to those of you who have lost loved ones. Undoubtedly this has left a deep hole in your heart.

To be sure, we are blessed to have the best medical technology in the world and a vaccine to cure and stop the spread of this dreaded disease is either here or well on its way. I look forward to the time, and I am sure you do too, when this Pandemic is past and will only be a distant memory.

If there is one thing this book does it is to give hope to those who would like a fresh start and a new beginning. It is perfect for recovering addicts, those whose mate has died, those going through divorce, those who have lost a job or had a business failure, or anyone who wants a better life. God Bless, Jim

P. S. When life hands you a lemon, you make lemonade.

Table of Contents

Preface

"Living on a hope and a Prayer"
"Take Life One Day at a Time."

E ach chapter of life holds a particular blessing. As a baby boomer from Pike County in Southern Arkansas, life was often tough along the Caddo River. We barely survived the droughts of 1953 and 1954. Though the Dust Bowl was more severe just west of us, cotton, corn, and cattle had no bottom in price and yields were worse than that. We hung on with a hope and a prayer. We ate what we could get and mother could always seem to manage a meal. Thankfully, we were able to hold onto the family farm when Dad went to work with the Arkansas State Police in Little Rock, Arkansas, in 1954.

I love Jim's compilation of simple yet helpful reminders of how to live life. It's as if Jim Davidson had spent time on my family farm to have put this book's thoughts and contents together. Even if Jim didn't live in my neck of the woods, he seemingly was influenced by the same people that I have known the past 74 years.

This book helped me remember that the best things in **life are free.** For instance, observing a child's growth, running through the rain, playing with a dog, smiling at others, or taking children to church to learn about God's salvation. Some of my favorite memories are watching my children sing "Nothing But the Blood of Jesus," or learning about how Jesus turned the water into wine. These are all integral parts of my life that cost nothing.

I just wish I had read this book 50 years ago.

Jim's book reminds me to get rid of the past. Work on the present and establish a foundation for your future. You can overvalue what we have now and then miss out on what really matters. This book and "The Author" will show you a better way.

This book helped me define "A hope and a prayer" with knowledge, temperance, diligence and brotherly kindness that are all in God's plan for life and developing relationships with others— especially your children, grandchildren, and the people you work with and serve.

I have spent more than 50 years building relationships. Many are still present today and I'm working to build more every day. I always ask four questions to start a good relationship. First, "Can I trust you?" Next, "Do you trust me?" Third, "Do you care about me? Lastly, "Will you keep me informed?" If all answers are "Yes," the relationship will last a lifetime. Always keep the lines of communication open both up and down because it helps relationships grow and be a resource for others.

Today, I am getting closer to the end of this slippery slope of life. I can only trust, wish and hope that I might hear some young person say, "There goes the man that showed me the way." There will be nothing better than that for me.

I know you will grow from reading this book. I will guarantee it. Jim Davidson is for real and lives what he writes. I know that stress is tough, but worry is a sin. "Rejoice in the Lord always and again I say rejoice. Let your moderation be known to all men. The Lord is at hand." Philippians 4:4-5.

I am honored and proud that I got to review "My Future Begins Today." I believe you will enjoy this book immensely.

Reviewed By: Jim Bob Baker
Faulkner County Judge
A Mule Rider from the Sixties
A Bull Shipper forever

Introduction

"A View from the Crow's Nest"

In the days before the invention of radar, satellites and mechanical power, all ships that ploughed the seas had something called a Crow's Nest. The Crow's Nest was "a structure or platform in the upper part of the main mast of a ship that was used as a lookout point." This position ensured the best view for a lookout to spot approaching storms, hazards, other ships or land by the naked eye. It was the best solution for this purpose until the invention of radar.

As I began to think about how I wanted to begin this book, this little allegory came to mind. The reason the Crow's Nest was important in those days is because the person perched high in a Crow's Nest had the advantage of a clear view of his surroundings. Similarly, I also have an advantage, as I am now more than 80 years of age and can pass on some of what life has taught me and what I have learned along the way. Over the past several years I have said many times, "I just wish I knew back when I was growing up what I know now." If you are an older person, you probably have made this comment as well.

You will be pleased to know that I am not a preacher and I don't try to preach, but I am a committed Christian and the ideas and concepts that I share are based on Biblical principles. This is simply to say that they have stood the test of time. What I am going to share about my background is never meant to boast or brag, as anything I have accomplished is to the Glory of God. I grew up in a small town in Southeast Arkansas with parents of modest means. We had a small restaurant and lived in four rooms in the back of it. The kids called our restaurant the "greasy spoon." They said it was the only restaurant in the state that was so bad the flies tried to get out.

Back in those days, I lived and breathed to play football and basketball. I thought I was good enough to attend college, play basketball and become a coach. No way, I could not even make the team. After a year and a half of my parents paying my tuition by selling 10-cent hamburgers, I dropped out of college and made my way to Little Rock where I had relatives. I soon took a job at a printing company earning $1.35 per hour.

I did this for seven years, working hard and learning the business well. When I left this company, I took a job in sales with another printer.

I would spend the next five years working my way up, on straight commission, to $25,000 per year. This was a lot of money in those days. I learned that a positive attitude and hard work pay off, as the president of this printing company took a liking to me and began to promote me in the Little Rock business community. I was involved in the Little Rock Chamber of Commerce, elected and served on the Pulaski County Quorum Court, was chairman of the Speakers Bureau of the United Way, and was active in a local church.

In 1968 I decided to take the Dale Carnegie Public Speaking Course. At the end of the 14-week course, I was selected to receive the "Leadership Gavel" as leader of the class. Two years later, my Dale Carnegie instructor asked me to go into business with him to distribute the Earl Nightingale Attitude Motivation programs that were produced on cassette. We started Motivation Services Inc. on May 1, 1970, and May 1, 2020, was my Golden Anniversary of being in the business of helping people succeed.

Soon after we started Motivation Services Inc., I learned that schools were my best prospects. "Attitude" was the buzz word for educators back in the 1970s, and they welcomed me with open arms. During this decade I would speak to more than 500 school facilities, dozens of student bodies,

Jim Davidson

and at numerous commencements and educational conferences. I would also conduct more than 50 six-hour "How to Plan Your Life" seminars with high school seniors, teaching them about career planning and the wonderful opportunities they had in the American Free Enterprise System. I also told them that they lived in the greatest country in the history of the world, and implored them to make sure they became good citizens and to always vote.

In 1980, due to the success of Earl Nightingale's "Our Changing World" radio program, I made the decision to begin my own radio program as well. Because of my school experience, I named it "How to Plan Your Life". Thanks to my acquired sales ability—I had been named "Salesman of the Year in Arkansas" in 1974—the list of radio subscribers grew to more than 300 stations coast to coast. Another exciting event occurred in 1995 when I began a syndicated newspaper column in my hometown newspaper, the Log Cabin Democrat, in Conway, Arkansas.

Again, fate smiled on me and over the next six to eight years the list of subscribers running my column grew to more than 365 newspapers in 35 states. From what I've been told by newspaper professionals, my column may be the most successful self-syndicated column in the history of American journalism. To date, I have written more than 1,300 columns and recently published a collection of 60 of the best columns in a book titled, *"Better than the Best."* It has been my good fortune to publish nine other books, make more than 1,700 speeches and be blessed more than anyone deserves.

However, I have saved the best for last. In 2005, along with a committee of my fellow citizens, we started an all-volunteer literacy project here in Conway titled, the Conway Bookcase Project. We give personalized oak bookcases and a starter set of books to preschool children being reared in low-income families. Now in our 16th year, this is an all giving-back project and no one earns a penny for their good work. To date, we have given more than 800 bookcases here in our community, and this has definitely changed lives. Thanks to a 2011 cover article in *American Profile* magazine (it had a circulation of more than 10 million), we now have projects in five other states, with a combined total of more than 2,800 bookcases given nationwide.

It is my sincere hope and prayer that this book will be a tremendous help to you over the coming months and years. I will say on the front end that I felt it was important for you to know my background and why I am uniquely qualified to write a book of this nature. You will discover very soon that this book is really about you, your life, your success and your happiness. It is meant to teach you, or at least remind you, of some truths, principles and concepts that can make a real difference in your future. If you think about it, ***"Your Future Begins Today"*** is so true. Yesterday and the past are gone. All we have is today, and we are not guaranteed another day, but we can profit from the past and plan for the future.

Sadly, there are millions of people in our great country today who let the mistakes and conflicts of the past keep them from being happy and making plans for a rewarding and exciting future. One thing I can promise is that you will have a different perspective when you finish this book. Please consider me to be your friend because I love people and my greatest joy comes from helping others.

God bless,
Jim Davidson

Begin with a Clean Slate

It has been said that an honest confession is good for the soul. I certainly hope this is true because I am about to confess. Quite often after being introduced to an audience, the first thing I say is that I am "just a sinner who has been saved by God's Amazing Grace." The Bible says in Romans 3:23, "For we have all sinned and come short of the glory of God." This verse is true, like the entire Bible, because this is the nature with which we were all born. I am sure you know the story of Adam and Eve that took place in the Garden of Eden. We are all sinners, and this includes you. We all make choices, do things and say things that we regret later on. There is something that happened in my life almost 40 years ago that made a tremendous difference. This has helped me wipe the slate clean, and I wanted to share it with you as you may be on the same road I was traveling.

Going back to the days when I was in high school, I went to church mainly because it was where the girls were. Later, as I moved out into the world, the church was still very important to me. At this time, like millions of Americans, I thought

I was a Christian, but I really did not know what this meant, other than being faithful to attend and supporting the church financially.

My good fortune came back in 1984 when I was saved during a revival meeting. I came to realize that all those years I had just been playing church, and was not a true born-again Christian. This is to say that I asked Jesus to come into my heart to be my personal Lord and Savior. I can tell you truthfully that since that day, February 26, 1984, my life has never been the same. It was not long after being saved that I began to think about the people over the years that I had wronged, cheated, or hurt in some way. I sought these people out and asked them to forgive me, and I also asked God to forgive me.

Now, I have titled these opening thoughts "Begin with a Clean Slate" as far as *Your Future Begins Today,* because we don't need to carry any unnecessary baggage that will slow us down or clutter our mind. We just need to be free to face each new day with hope and optimism, and make exciting plans that will make our future brighter than it's ever been. Here is what I discovered that has made all the difference for me. Soon after I was saved in that revival meeting, I was asked to teach a young boy's Sunday school class. I accepted the invitation, but it did not take me long to realize that I did not know the Bible.

In an attempt to learn the Bible, I made the decision to read the Bible all the way through in a year. Would you believe that I continued this regimen each year for the next 25 years straight? To the glory of God, needless to say I now know the Bible pretty well. I have many verses memorized and they have helped me tremendously. One that comes to mind is Psalm 119:-11 which says, "Thy Word I have hid in my heart that I might not sin against thee."

However, there is one special verse that I want to share with you because it relates to what I was saying earlier about asking God to forgive me of my sins. The verse I am referring to is I John 1:9. It says, "If we confess our sins, He is faithful and just to forgive our sins, and cleanse us from all unrighteousness." The two key words here are "forgive" and "cleanse."

As a born-again believer, when we sincerely confess our sins, He says they are cast as far as the east is from the west. The reason is because my sins are now covered by His precious blood that was shed for me when He hung on the old rugged cross. Now, that is special and is available to anyone who will come to Him and place their hope and trust in Him.

Now, to be sure, I could have left this portion out of the book, but that would have been a great disservice for every reader who is burdened with a load of guilt, like me, and does not know how to be forgiven and have the slate wiped clean. We all make mistakes. The only people who do not make them are in the cemetery. But Praise God, by knowing I John 1:9, we can ask for forgiveness when we sin, hurt other people and make mistakes. As time passes, our sins and mistakes will come further and further apart. I can promise you—this is the best way to live and have a happy and more satisfying life. It is so true: *YOUR FUTURE BEGINS TODAY*.

The Toddler, Teenage & Young Adult Years

From Birth to Age 30

S everal years ago, someone wrote a great prayer for a public speaker. It goes, "Lord, fill my mouth with worthwhile stuff, and nudge me when I have said enough." This is the same admonition that I will use in writing this book. Here is my suggestion to help you get the most from the investment of time that you will be making. First, don't be in a hurry. Take some time as you read each chapter, meditate on it and reflect on how what I am saying could benefit and help you.

As you advance in years, you will discover that you also need some quiet time alone to think about your goals and how you plan to achieve them. Here is what works for me during my quiet time each morning: I begin with prayer and then read *My Daily Scripture Devotional* that was given to me by my wife Janis. Next, I read a short devotional that was written by a chaplain who served our nation in Afghanistan and was always in harm's way. This reminds me to be grateful for those who helped secure and preserve our freedom. It is so very encouraging.

Then, I read two radio transcripts from my book titled, *The Best of Jim Davidson,* "a collection of my radio transcripts. Since there are only 60 of these in the book, I can read it all the way through in a month's time. Then, I also read a couple of selections from my book, *Better Than the Best,* which contains 60 columns from more than 1,300 that I have written. Both of these books are motivational in nature and they help to seed my mind with positive thoughts. Along with my devotional, this is a perfect way to begin the day.

There are three keys to learning. The first is repetition. The second is repetition. The third is repetition.

I read my two books from six to 10 times each year because of something I learned several years ago. Princeton University conducted a study, and they learned that a message read or heard one time was completely washed out of the mind 24 hours later. However, a message read or heard several times a day for eight days was practically memorized, and 30 days later the mind retained 90 percent of the message. This helped me realize why repetition is so very important.

Now, let's move on and talk about the first 10 chapters in the book as we look at the "Toddler, Teenage and Young Adult Years." The first chapter is titled "Don't Shoot Yourself in the Foot," and this may be the most important bit of information that we will explore together. Get this one right and the chances of achieving great success and happiness have been increased immeasurably. Obviously, the toddler years will be directed to the child's parents, and today we need great parents more than ever in the history of our nation.

Next we will look at the teenage years which, again, are very important years. Parents will be most interested in the topics I cover that set the tone and direction for a great life and a great future. I am confident that a lot of young people will be reading this book as well, and there is one thing I can promise you: you will be the leaders of tomorrow in business, education, government, our military and all the other facets that make up the greatest nation in the history of the world.

And then, the young adult years—a time when important decisions will be made, such as school or college, a career, marriage, where you are going to live, and learning about financial planning. This is the wonderful thing about a book where we begin as a toddler and end in the third section with the legacy of a tremendously successful man or woman who has "done it right" and can look back with pride on the success they have achieved. I know there will be many highlights along the way, and a great number of nice things that will be said about you at your funeral. When my time comes, there is only one thing that I want on my tombstone, in addition to my name, date of my birth and death, and one verse of scripture, Philippians 4:13. I just want my tombstone to say: "He Made a Difference." I am sure you will have made a difference, too.

CHAPTER ONE
Don't Shoot Yourself in the Foot!

No one in their right mind would intentionally take a loaded gun and shoot themselves in the foot. The first consequence would be intense pain, then blood beginning to run everywhere, and when they couldn't get the bleeding stopped, a trip to the emergency room. After the hospital people checked him out and cleaned the wound, it would probably require surgery to repair the damage. Depending on whether he had insurance or not, a hefty medical bill would follow. The sad news is, this person may not be able to walk without pain again for as long as he lives.

The reason I have shared this story with you is because of the way the human mind is constituted. We remember things much longer when blood is involved and the story is graphic. And I want you to remember this story for as long as you live. There is a natural law here that controls everything in the universe. It is called the law of Cause and Effect—every cause has an effect and every effect has a cause.

There are many natural laws in existence, but the one that everyone knows is the law of gravity. If you get on top of a step ladder or a tall building and fall or walk off, you will always go down, you will never go up. This is the way all natural laws work and they literally control our lives. If you would like to know more, just go to the Internet and type "natural laws" in the search box, as there is lots of information there.

Here is the good news: When we know and understand how natural laws work, we are in a position to almost tell our own future, and maybe more importantly, to help our children and young adults avoid poor choices. Here is another thought for your sharp mind to think about: "We can choose our choices, but we cannot choose the consequences of our choices." It is really quite simple: when we make good choices, the law is working for us, and when we make bad choices, the law is working against us.

Here are some choices that I have made that work for me: I don't use drugs, smoke, drink alcohol, use profanity, run with immoral or ungodly people, and I do my best to be honest, tell the truth and treat others as I wish to be treated.

Here is a good example in my own family of what happens when people make poor choices. We know from research that smoking cigarettes causes lung cancer. I have a sister and an uncle who started smoking when they were young. Both became addicted and became chain smokers. Sad to say, before their time, they both passed away from lung cancer, and I am sure they were in some pain before they left us.

The term "shoot yourself in the foot" has been used so often that it has become a cliché. In our modern language it means anything we do or say that is not in our own best interest is simply shooting ourselves in the foot. Now, I am sure you are sharp and you get the picture, and I hope you can use this information. If you have children, teach it to them as well. One reason I am so excited about this book and the information that follows is that the title, *Your Future Begins Today,* means that your past is gone, and today we can all make the choice to have a better, happier and more successful life.

We see people all the time who do bad things and think they can get away with it. They may get away with it for a while, but remember that the law always works and consequences can come back to haunt them, usually at a most inopportune time. As this relates to rearing our children, here is something that we should constantly be aware of if our children are to be successful adults. The most important and crucial time in the life of a young child is from birth to about the age of 5. It's during this time that he or she learns to walk and talk, and also begins the process of developing his or her own unique personality. The most important people in a child's life are his parents. As American clergyman Henry Ward Beecher said, "A mother is the child's school room." Any child is indeed blessed if he or she is born into a family and home with two parents who are educated, financially stable, and who have reared other successful children. We know in today's society this is not the case a high percentage of the time, as the divorce rate is around 50 percent and the culture is not, for the most part, family friendly.

I had a personal experience several years ago that may be of value to you. In the days when I was teaching a "How to Plan Your Life" seminar to high school students, after we had spent some time together and I had earned their trust, I would explain the law of Cause and Effect in considerable detail. Then I would tell them that when they did things that were morally or ethically wrong and even unlawful, this great principle that affects us all was working against them and not for them. The consequences of their actions will be either good or bad. At this point I would look them straight in the eye and say, "I really care about you, but from this day forward you can never say that you were not told."

We must teach our children these important truths for them to have any hope of succeeding later in life. This is simply teaching character to those we love the most. Most parents love their children, but quite often they do not teach them how to succeed, and they don't really understand why it is important for them to be a good role model. Children emulate their parents more by what they see and not so much by what they hear. The children who are being reared in today's culture are in a war for their very souls. A great book on parenting that I can highly recommend is ***Battle-Ready Moms Raising Battle-Ready Kids***, by Reba Bowman.

CHAPTER TWO

The Gift of Great Parents!

Sometime back I read a wonderful book titled, *Uncommon,* written by Coach Tony Dungy. A former college and NFL player, he later coached the Tampa Bay Buccaneers and the Indianapolis Colts. He and his staff took the Colts to the Super Bowl in 2007. He became the first African-American coach to win the Super Bowl and have his players experience the thrill of being world champions. However, I was more impressed with his personal life and the tremendous role model he has become than anything he ever did on the football field. As I read, *Uncommon,* I could clearly see the reason for his outstanding success in both areas of his life. It can be summed up in two words: sterling parents. Both of his parents were outstanding people and outstanding citizens. They not only taught young Tony through their words, but also by the way they lived. This had a profound effect on the coach's character and, ultimately, on his success.

While still in their formative years, a child will develop many of the habits and attitudes of his or her parents. The child will grow up and remain in the same church, the same political party, and often the same line of work. This is a general statement because I understand that times have changed. Today, the majority of American young people are not attending church and there is an upheaval in the political realm. The rise of the welfare state distorts all values that are the underpinnings of the American Free Enterprise System. With the age of technology, career choices have shifted dramatically over the past several years. Just remember that facts and statistics change, but principles do not.

Here is the good news/bad news part of what I am saying, at least for the child growing up in today's complex world. We cannot choose our parents any more than we can choose the color of our skin, where we were born, and whether or not our parents are educated or financially successful. We are born into an environment and, for the most part, we are shaped and molded without the power to choose until later in life. If we draw a lucky number and win the parent lottery, we have a head start. If not, we have challenges that may be difficult, if not impossible, to overcome. Many parents, especially those who do not understand the law of Cause and Effect, have bad personal habits that are picked up by their children, and this hinders their chance for success. It's a price no child should have to pay. It's an established fact that the majority of people in our society today who smoke do so because their parents smoked. They drink because their parents drank, gamble because their parents gambled, use profanity because their parents used profanity, use drugs because their parents used drugs, view pornography because their parents viewed pornography, and have many other destructive habits because their parents did. There is no doubt that most parents love their children and make all kinds of personal sacrifices for them. They do this while never realizing that their own personal habits will be millstones around the necks of their children for as long as they live. What I am saying can be summed up in this story by Jack R. Griffin titled "The Education of Johnny O. Muddle." Did you hear about the young man named Johnny O. Muddle who was kicked out of a service academy? He was 19 when he was caught cheating, but his problems really began much earlier. When he was 6 years old, he was with his father when they were caught speeding. His father handed the officer a $10 bill with his driver's license. "It's OK, Son," his father said as they drove off. "Everybody does it." When he was 8, he was at a family council presided over by Uncle George, on the surest means to shave points off the income tax return. "It's OK, Kid," his uncle said. "Everybody does it." When he was 9, his mother took him to see his first theater production. The box office man couldn't find any seats until his mother discovered an extra 20 dollars in her purse. "It's OK, Son," she said "Everybody does it." When he was 12, he broke his glasses on the way to school. His Aunt Francine persuaded the insurance company they had been stolen and they collected $75. "It's OK, Kid," she said. "Everybody does it." When he was 15, he made right guard on the high school football team. His coach showed him how to block and at the same time grab the opposing end by the shirt so the official couldn't see it. "It's OK, Kid," the coach said. "Everybody does it." When he was 16, he took a summer job at the big market. His assignment was to put the over-ripe tomatoes in the bottom of the boxes and the good ones on the top where they would show. "It's OK, Kid," the manager said. "Everybody does it." When he was 17, his older brother Lance, who was just less than seven feet tall, studied offers from 21 universities who needed a tall center. He selected the one that offered the biggest down payment on a new car and gave a scholarship to his girlfriend Gertrude. It's OK, Kid," the recruiter said. "Everybody does it." When he was 18, he and a neighbor applied for an opening at a service academy. Johnny was a marginal student. His neighbor was in the upper 3 percent of his class but he couldn't play right guard. Johnny got the assignment. "It's OK, Kid," they told him, "Everybody does it." When he was 19, he was approached by an upper classman who offered him the test answers for $10. "It's OK, Kid," he said. "Everybody does it."

Johnny was caught and sent home in disgrace! How could you do this to your mother and me?" his father said, "You never learned anything like this at home."

"The youth of today are failing," said the psychiatrist. "They refuse to determine the difference between right and wrong."

"More than 50 percent of our students are cheats," said the educator. "It's shameful the way young people carry on today."

"The youth of today are setting a pattern that is alarming. We've got to get those bums cleaned out," said the commandant of the academy. "And now we can walk tall."

And here is the sad commentary: "If there is one thing the adult world can't stand it's a kid who cheats." An old saying applies here: The fruit does not fall far from the tree. When it comes to rearing our children, they are influenced more by what they see than by what they hear. Many parents in today's society were not reared in homes where traditional moral, ethical, and spiritual values were taught, so they don't practice them. However, there is one thing we can count on: if we don't influence our children for good, someone else will influence them for bad. As we look to the future, it would behoove all of us—as parents, grandparents, teachers, coaches and others who influence children—to be or become good mentors and good role models. The future of our nation literally hangs in the balance. Sometimes it is as important to have confirmed what we already know as it is to learn new things. This came to mind when I read a newspaper article recently about a study which identified and ranked the top 10 parenting skills. You and I both could have listed most of them ourselves, but it is comforting to have confirmed—as well as emphasized—what we already know. For reference, the researchers are Robert Epstein and Shannon Fox, and their findings were reported in the November/ December 2010 issue of *Scientific American Mind*.

Here are the top 10 parenting skills, without comments, listed from most to least important.

No. 1: Love and Affection
No. 2: Stress Management
No. 3: Relationship Skills
No. 4: Autonomy and Independence
No. 5: Education and Learning
No. 6: Life Skills
No. 7: Behavior Management
No. 8: Health
No. 9: Religion
No. 10: Safety

No doubt about it: America's greatest resource is her children.

CHAPTER THREE
Mommy, Please Read to Me!

We hear a lot these days about school dropouts and what causes this to happen to so many students. In some parts of our nation, the number is as high as four out of every 10 students who start school in kindergarten and never walk down the aisle to get a high school diploma. There are also vast numbers of students who walk across the stage to the familiar refrain of "Pomp & Circumstance," but who can barely read, if at all, the diploma they are given. The answer to this dilemma may be a lot simpler than many people realize. The key to reading, learning and success in school largely depends on the student's vocabulary, especially in the early years of a child's life.

Sometime back, researchers at a major university took students in a graduating class, gave them an English vocabulary test and then tracked them for 20 years. Not surprisingly, those who knew the definitions of the most words were in the highest income group 20 years later. The researchers also discovered that the people who, in the beginning, had the worst vocabulary scores were in the lowest income group two decades later. Now, here is something that should give all of us a reason to give pause. **There was not a single exception.** It is important to note that the students in this study were college graduates. How about the millions of students who graduate from high school but never enroll in an institution of higher learning? And, let's go a little lower on the scale. How about the millions of students who drop out of high school and never graduate?

If one or more of these students happens to be your child or grandchild, do you have any idea what kind of life he or she will have in our society as a high school dropout? In the vast majority of cases, high school dropouts face a life of much lower income, even if they can find a job, and this leads to all kinds of problems for society. We are all affected by high school dropouts whether we know it or not, and whether we like it or not. One of the primary reasons American schools are struggling today is the change that has taken place over several decades in the parents' reading habits. A study found that in 1955, 81 percent of parents read to or with their children. Today that number is around 21 percent. We know that parents must be involved in the education of their children for them to succeed in school, but that involvement must begin much earlier in the home.

Needless to say, children who come from homes where reading and education are priorities have a tremendous advantage over children who come from homes where there are few books and where parents read to them. So, back to the subject at hand, "Mommy Please Read to Me." If you are a parent, grandparent or other responsible person in the life of a toddler or preschool child, please consider seriously what I am saying. You could never spend any more productive and satisfying time than to get a few good children's books and read to your preschool child or children. Just find a good time during the day when you can do this, and before long your child, if you are the mother, will come to you and say, "Mommy, please read to me?" What a blessing this will be to know that you are building the foundation for a great future.

We have a terrific school superintendent who is retiring this year but has been a great supporter of our Bookcase for Every Child project. One year, Dr. Greg Murry was the keynote speaker for our annual awards ceremony, and he had this to say: "Disadvantaged first-graders have a vocabulary of 2,900 words, while other students have twice that many. It is important for parents who have school-age children to have books, bookshelves and bookcases in their homes." When it comes to developing a good vocabulary, which is paramount for success, Dr. Murry stated that the out-of-school reading habits of students have shown that even 15 minutes a day of independent reading can expose students to more than a million words of text in a year. That is impressive.

Now, here is where we need to really get serious. The children who are at the greatest risk are those being reared in low-income homes. We know this is true, but the reason the majority of these students do not develop a good vocabulary when they are young is because their parents can't read. According to the Right to Read Foundation, there are 42 million American adults who can't read at all and millions more who are marginal. As previously stated, 81 percent of parents read to or with their children in 1955 when literacy rates were much higher. Today that number is around 21 percent. Based on what I reported earlier about the university study that found that vocabulary and income were so closely linked, it should be obvious that those who really need help are those with lower incomes, thus the reason for our bookcase project.

This leads to a logical conclusion—illiteracy and poverty are generational. If we can break the cycle of illiteracy with young children, it will have a great impact for generations to come. We have something in our state (and I am sure in all other states) called the Arkansas Literacy Council. This council has a small staff and volunteers who work with adults, and they are certainly helping a lot of these people. We also have another resource in our country that many people may not know about. A former teacher, principal and school administrator by the name of Dr. Ruby Payne started a company several years ago called "Aha! Process, Inc." This company works with all kinds of organizations to help them understand the effects of poverty on students, families and communities, and how to support people from all economic backgrounds. Her great book, *"A Framework for Understanding Poverty,"* should be required reading for any person who leads and inspires others, especially as these endeavors relate to literacy.

CHAPTER FOUR

The Rewards of Good Habits!

Our habits and values define who we are as a person. This is because what is taking place on the inside—our mind, our heart and our spirit—shows up on the outside as our behavior and actions for others to see. Even if no one else sees what we are doing, our subconscious mind sees, because we can never escape from ourselves. Wherever we go, we are always there. Because our habits and our values are so closely related, I have grouped them together but will make some clear distinctions as we go along.

To make sure we are speaking the same language, let me define these two phrases. First, our personal habits: According to the dictionary, a habit is "an act or practice so frequently repeated as to become almost automatic." A good example is when we brush our teeth. Most of us have done this so long and so often that we don't have to be reminded to learn how, we just subconsciously do it one or more times each day.

Psychologists tell us it takes 21 days to form a new habit. We must decide on the new habit we wish to form, repeat it several times each day for 21 straight days and it will become a habit. Then, we will repeat the action without having to think about it. However, if we miss one day in the process, we must go back, begin again, and go 21 more days for the action to be firmly fixed in our subconscious mind.

When it comes to achieving personal success, here is something we all need to know and understand. An insurance executive from Philadelphia by the name of Albert E. N. Gray discovered the common denominator of success: Forming the habit of doing things that people who fail don't like to do. Self-discipline, hard work, setting goals, developing a service attitude, and striving to improve are not the provinces of a failure. To say it very simply, when we deliberately form good habits, they work to our advantage (remember the law of cause and effect) while bad habits we form work to defeat us. As the famous educator Horace Mann has said, "A habit is a cable. We weave a thread of it every day, and at last we cannot break it."

Now, let's talk about personal values. According to the dictionary, a value is "something regarded as desirable, worthy or right, as a belief, standard or moral precept." While life is far too complex to reduce to a list, it will be helpful in circumstances where they apply to have the following checklist of personal values to gauge how well we are doing. This list is certainly not exhaustive but, as in the case of habits, our values must personify the good or right side of any action or activity in which we are involved. Otherwise, as I have said before, we would just be shooting ourselves in the foot.

Respect: this is the basis and the foundation for all successful human relationships. While we don't have to agree with another person, like them, or approve of their actions or lifestyle, we must respect them as another human being who, in the eyes of God, has great worth and value. Please take this comment for what it is worth. As the English poet Samuel Coleridge said, "Advice is like snow: the softer it falls, and the longer it is dwelt upon, the deeper it sinks into the mind."

Honesty: It has been said that honesty is looking painful truths in the face. Honesty is much more than returning lost money to its rightful owner, not cheating on our income taxes, or not stealing from our employer. In today's society, it is a rare quality, but yet one which every employer is looking for in an employee. The person who is taught honesty from birth will go the extra mile to do the right thing and to make sure the other person is not shortchanged in a deal. To be sure, those who develop reputations for honesty will be the benefactors of all kinds of rewards, and they will be happy with themselves, which is the greatest happiness of all.

Truthfulness: When I watch the news on television or read an editorial in the newspaper, the question that often comes to my mind is: Are they telling the truth? It's been said that we should be willing to throw our most cherished beliefs in the trash if we can find something that comes closer to the truth. I will confess that many times what someone is saying and what I believe to be the truth are miles apart. Dr. Dennis Waitley, famous speaker and writer, has helped to clear this up for me. He said, "The mind has an amazing quality. It doesn't automatically gravitate toward truth, right, justice and ... the best. It gravitates toward what it is exposed to the most."

Dependability: This important personal value simply means that we will do what we say we will do. We all know people who are not dependable, and it does not take long to figure out which ones they are. This quality extends to every area of our lives and every moment we are awake. There are thousands of people in our nation today who lose their jobs because they don't bother to come to work for two or three days and don't call to explain why, or they are always late. These people are simply not dependable. Again, this is a quality that must be taught to our children. At our age, my wife and I have weeded out most of the people who are not dependable. When our friends say they are coming to dinner at 6 o'clock, we can have the ice in the glasses. It is far better to say that we will not do something than to say we will and then not do it. At least be honest with yourself and admit you won't do something.

Responsibility: When the chips are down, or even when they are up, the responsible person will step up and say, "I made a mistake," or "It was my fault, and I take full responsibility for it." This person will not engage in the blame game or pass the buck when it was his or her responsibility to do a job or take care of something. We all make mistakes and it is important to learn from our mistakes. We won't learn if we are not a responsible person. This is a quality that must be taught, especially when a child is young. Otherwise, they will go through life looking for an easy route, or a way out, and never mature as a human being. And responsibility isn't just taking the blame (or credit) for something. It also means accepting and doing something because it is expected of you and may not even be a part of your job.

Loyalty: The American writer and publisher Elbert Hubbard once said, "An ounce of loyalty is worth a pound of cleverness." Many people are loyal to a fault, and this is a quality to be admired. However, this makes it even more important to have a good understanding of human nature, and to pledge our loyalty or choose to work with people who have character and integrity. For example, if we are loyal to a bank robber, we may go down when they go down. There is an old saying that blood is thicker than water, and being loyal to our relatives is admirable. However, if you even suspect poor character, dishonesty or trouble with the law, let them know up front that you will not help them break the law or lie for them.

Persistence: Former President Calvin Coolidge is credited with this famous saying: "Press on—nothing in the world can take the place of persistence. Talent will not; nothing is more common than unsuccessful men with talent. Genius will not; unrewarded genius is almost a proverb. Education will not; the world is full of educated derelicts. Persistence and determination alone are omnipotent." The reason the vast majority of people in our nation are unsuccessful is because they quit too soon. I have seen this happen many times in my own life and career. I call it the "Bulldog Factor." When you get ahold of something that is truly important, act like a bulldog and don't let it go. Keep going. The skies will clear and you will achieve success unrealized in the common hour.

Courage: Sir Winston Churchill, former Prime Minister of the United Kingdom, once said, "Courage is that quality of mind or spirit enabling one to meet danger or opposition with fearlessness, calmness and firmness. It is the quality that guarantees all others." There are many forms of courage. Winston Churchill lived in a time when his nation was engaged in a battle for its very survival. This is the same kind of courage that rises to the occasion when a man's family is attacked by animals or other human beings. It also takes courage to take a stand for what a person believes in, to stand up when others stay seated, and to speak up when others are quiet. We should weigh our odds carefully. There is a time to have courage, and there are other times when we should run away and live to fight another day.

Forgiveness: In the Bible, Jesus is asked by a man if he should forgive someone seven times, which is the number for completion or perfection. Jesus replied, "No, 70 times seven." He was saying that we must forgive someone as many times as they ask us. This is one of the hardest things for many people to do—to forgive someone who has hurt them deeply, and caused injury or even death in some cases. Yet anger, bitterness and resentment will eat us alive if we don't forgive those who have wronged us. If we will simply trust God and know that in due time the transgressor will suffer the consequences for wrongdoing, we can find peace in our heart and a life worth living. By not forgiving a person who did you wrong, that person continues to cause you pain and suffering until you let go. It is not that they deserve forgiveness, but that you deserve peace.

There are two words in the English language that will summarize what I have been saying from the very beginning. These words are **character** and **integrity.** We all know men and women who have sterling character, and as a result have developed an excellent reputation. As Abraham Lincoln said, "Character is like a tree and reputation is like its shadow." For any person so blessed, this did not happen by accident, and it certainly did not happen overnight. Rather, it was the early years of deliberate training by wise and understanding parents, or some other successful person, who taught this person character values by precept and example.

"Character is the total of thousands of small daily strivings, to live up to the best that is in us ... the final decision to reject whatever is demeaning to oneself or to others and with confidence and honesty to choose the right."
—American Army General Arthur G. Trudeau

CHAPTER FIVE

Attitude is Really Gratitude!

In 1970, I went into business with my former Dale Carnegie instructor—the late Bob Gannaway—to sell the Earl Nightingale success motivation programs on cassette. This was about the time the cassette player came along and long before the compact disc revolutionized the recording industry.

After only a few weeks in business, we discovered that the best prospects for our motivation programs were our public and private schools, because "attitude" had become the "buzz" word among our nation's educators. In our Arkansas schools, we found many willing buyers of our programs. We were also given the opportunity to speak to countless groups, both staff and students, in a variety of settings. Some 10 years after I started working with our schools, I did a quick count and found that I had addressed more than 500 school faculties, most K-12, at their preschool workshops. No doubt, this is where I developed my passion for literacy.

It was during this time that I traveled more than 50,000 miles each year and spent countless hours in my car. Since the motivational recordings were on cassette, I had a cassette player installed in my car. At the time I never dreamed this would be the key for me to get an education on principles and concepts that would serve me well for the rest of my life. As an aside, I highly recommend this valuable use of time in our cars—a university on wheels. There are hundreds of motivational, inspirational and learning tapes and CDs available for your continuing education. You can learn while you ride, rather than listen to music or a rehash of the news.

As I listened repeatedly to the same messages week after week, I had the opportunity to bring the best widely known motivational speakers right into the cabin of my car. These men and women not only had the effect of inspiring me, but their life-changing principles were instilled in the recesses of my subconscious mind. The message from the Nightingale series that everyone loved the most was called, "The Magic Word." That magic word is "attitude." Since those early days I have come to understand and appreciate the power that our own attitudes have over our lives.

Attitude has been defined as a "position or bearing as indicating action, feeling or mood." This means that our actions actually trigger our feelings, and our feelings also trigger our actions. Many times I have been reluctant to do my exercises, but went ahead anyway, and my feelings changed dramatically once I got started. Now, this question please: "Do you know people who have a great attitude?" Please ponder that question for a moment. Here is what William James of Harvard University had to say about attitude. Dr. James, known as the father of American psychology, said, "The greatest discovery of my generation is that human beings can alter their lives by altering their attitudes of mind."

Recent studies have revealed that attitude is responsible for about 85 percent of our success, while skill and knowledge make up the balance. In spite of this, most classes in schools and colleges across the nation spend far more time teaching skills and knowledge than they do attitude. I see the effect of attitude all the time when I shop in some of our local stores. Most employees who are drawing a paycheck have no idea of the power of their own attitude and how developing a positive, helpful attitude could get them promotions, raises, higher commissions, return customers, and all kinds of benefits that otherwise might quietly pass them by.

Sometimes when I encounter an employee with an expressionless face or no acknowledgment that I am shopping at their store, I want to say, "What are you working for?" Until and unless they change their attitude, they are just relegating themselves to the bottom of the economic ladder as long as they live. On the other hand, every so often I encounter someone who truly understands the importance of a positive attitude and they are courteous, friendly and helpful. You just know they have a much brighter future than 95 percent of the other employees. The only difference is their attitude.

The truth is, people do business with people they like and who make them feel welcome and appreciated. The late Dale Carnegie taught a principle in his famous self-improvement courses that will help any of us, regardless of what we do for a living, or even if we happen to be retired. "You can make more friends in two months by becoming interested in other people than you can in two years by trying to get other people interested in you," he taught. This quote reminds me of the conceited nurse: she always subtracted 10 beats from her patient's pulse to compensate for her own good looks and the effects of her personality.

It can truthfully be said that when it comes to rising to the top in a job, career, marriage or most anything you care to name, "it's your attitude and not your aptitude that will determine your altitude." In the future, as you encounter people each day, just remember that they all have an invisible sign across their chest that says, "Make Me Feel Important." Do this in a sincere way, on a regular basis, and you will be blessed beyond measure by the benefits and rewards that will come your way. As the old saying goes, "You can catch more flies with honey than you can with vinegar."

There is a story about a lady who constantly complained about her neighbors: their grass was too tall, their kids where too rowdy, their cars were always filthy and everything else was unacceptable. She really had a negative and pessimistic attitude. Then one day she washed the windows in her own house—and the whole neighborhood cleared up. We all have bad days when things don't go right, but the time we spend working on our own attitude will be some of the most profitable we can ever spend. And I have saved the best for last. The more we develop a great attitude, the more successful we will become, and with this comes a grateful heart for all the good things that have come our way. It is true: Attitude is really Gratitude.

CHAPTER SIX

You Set the Priorities!

Unlike when I was growing up back in the mid-1950s, today's youth have things competing for their time that tend to crowd out reading, especially out-of-school reading. In today's culture, our youth are bombarded with many forms of advertising that promotes the use of electronics as a way to stay connected, including the internet, Smartphones, Facebook, Twitter, and blogs. When it comes to using these devices, here is a question that we would all do well to think about: Are these companies using us, or are we using them? Well, the answer is they are using us. Their first priority is making money, and the future of our children will take a back seat every time.

We only have 24 hours each day, and it's up to us to determine how we use them. Here is a good example of what I am saying. Recently I heard on the national news that 85 percent of all teenagers take their Smartphones to bed with them and spend untold hours texting their friends. When a young person stays awake, texting most of the night, obviously the next day at school he or she feels like a zombie. Lack of sleep is a major contributor to poor grades, sleeping in class, traffic accidents, etc. This is without regard to the fact that teens and adults should get a minimum of seven hours of sleep per night.

Now, anyone with common sense knows this is not a healthy situation for millions of young people in our country, but the companies that are selling and promoting Smartphones and other devices to younger and younger prospects seem to ignore what they are doing to education. To restate the obvious, a child's education is tied directly to his or her ability to read. Further, to excel, a child must read well. Why do you think schools all across the nation are banning these electronic devices? We must teach our children about the harmful effects of these devices when they are very young, as early as age 2, 3, 4 and 5 years of age.

Now, please don't misunderstand what I am saying. I am not opposed to using modern inventions that will help us achieve greater success in our lives. Back in 1968, I was one of the first people in Little Rock, Arkansas, to have a telephone in my car. I worked in outside sales and it was very helpful to be able to call the company I was working for, or to call prospects, or to provide a way for my customers to get in touch with me. I was using the telephone to help me. I was not using it to help the telephone company. Sadly, too many young people are insecure and feel they must constantly stay in touch with friends, family and others. All the while, they are letting their valuable time slip by, and they will reap the consequences later in ways they can't even imagine. This does not even mention the fact that most young people can't spell these days, nor can they write in cursive, and often can't even carry on a simple conversation.

To say it very simply, devices can be good or they can be bad, depending on how we use them. To achieve greater success in our lives, we should be our own person and work on those things that will produce the kind of life that will be rewarding, and leave the kinds of things that waste time to those who are wasting their lives.

The late Earl Nightingale, who I knew personally, once said, "If you will watch what the crowd is doing and do exactly the opposite, you will probably never make another mistake as long as you live." Now, that is a thought that we would all do well to ponder for a long time. Of course, there are many other distractions to learning and reading. In America today we have a sports culture that ranks right up there with politics and the Weather Channel. Every day in America there are millions of young people who spend untold hours practicing and playing sports for fun and enjoyment. Only a very small percentage become good enough to make it to the next level—college and pro—and earn their living from sports. The truth is, if a child spends most of their time playing sports and does not spend time reading on a regular basis, they miss a multitude of opportunities that will come later.

Here is a terrific example of what I have been saying. It can be found in the true story of Dr. Ben Carson, who ran for president of the United States. He is the author of a fantastic book titled, *"Gifted Hands,"* and my information comes from this book.

As a child, Ben, an African-American, grew up with his mother and brother Curtis in the inner city of Detroit, Michigan. His mother and father divorced when he was only 7 years old, and Ben attended a mostly white school. He was doing poorly in elementary school and some of the other children began to call him "dummy". His mother got wind of it. She was working three jobs to make ends meet and she laid down the law to Ben and Curtis. She said, "You must read two books each week before you can go out and play or do anything else." The boys did not like it, but accepted her ultimatum because of their respect for her, knowing she was working three jobs just to support them.

Something else that is important is that Ben's mother, Sonja Carson, was doing cleaning and housework for some highly prominent people in the city. As a result, she was exposed to many cultural things that wealthy people do, such as listening to classical music, and attending plays, the theatre, and concerts, and many other aspects of the arts. In addition to having her sons read two books a week, she began to expose Ben and Curtis to these cultural things as well. In time, Ben began to excel in school. His grades were tops, and along about the ninth grade, many of the same kids who called him "dummy" back in elementary school began to come to him asking for help with their homework.

When Ben graduated from high school, he received a four-year scholarship to Yale University, where he graduated with honors. His dream was to become a doctor. After Yale, he applied for and was accepted to the Michigan School of Medicine. For his internship, he was accepted at Johns Hopkins in Baltimore, Maryland, where he was later the head of the department of Pediatric Neurosurgery. Then in 1987, Dr. Carson and a team of surgeons made history when they performed the first successful separation of conjoined twins who were connected at the head. It's a thrilling story about a disadvantaged child who was fortunate enough to have a mother like Sonja Carson, who laid down the law to him and made him read quality books at a very early age.

Sometimes all it takes to make a vast improvement is just to be reminded of things we know but sometimes have forgotten. As the parent, you set the priorities and this begins when a child is a toddler. Waiting until your child is 8 to 10 years of age may be too long, and because we failed to do our job, the child will suffer the consequences for the rest of their days. Just remember Dr. Ben Carson's story: he did not like it when his mother told them they "had" to read two books each week before they could go out to play or do other things. She had her sons' best interest at heart because she loved them and she knew that reading was a way for them to become successful.

CHAPTER SEVEN
Train Up Your Children!

In the 18th Century, a French Nobleman by the name of Alexis De Tocqueville came to our shores seeking to learn why America had become so powerful and so great in such a short period of time. After being here for several months, he came to a conclusion: "I searched for the greatness of America in her gleaming cities and her towering skyscrapers and it was not there. I searched for it in her fertile plains and massive rivers but it was not there. Not until I went to the churches of America and saw her pulpits aflame with righteousness did I understand the secret of her genius and power." He may or may not have known that seven of the eight present-day Ivy League colleges—Cornell being the exception—were founded to prepare ministers for teaching and preaching the Gospel.

When the 555-foot Washington Monument was constructed in our nation's capital of Washington, D.C., our forefathers had the Latin phrase "Laus Deo" inscribed on the eastern side of the aluminum capstone where the sun's rays strike it first. This phrase is only visible for Heaven to see, but it means, "Praise be to God." When it comes to planning their lives, many Americans leave out spirituality, seldom if ever darkening the doors of a church or synagogue. By doing so, in most cases, they are denying their children the opportunity to learn spiritual and moral values that would help them for the rest of their lives. Proverbs 22:6 says, "Train up a child in the way he should go and when he is old, he will not depart from it."

You do not have to look far in today's society to see examples where young people are making choices that lead them into drugs, crime, suicide, prison, teen pregnancy, and all manner of negative consequences. Much of this could have been avoided if parents had taught moral and spiritual values in their home. We have many different churches, denominations, and forms of religion. While I may not agree with some of them, I respect the rights of all people to worship as they please—or not worship at all. What I am sharing is from my heart, and 40-plus years of experience working with young people in a variety of settings. I just believe that our children deserve the best, and it's up to parents to provide it for them.

The self-discipline of spending quiet time each morning with the Lord, having prayer time and Bible reading has made a difference for me. Now, each choice or decision I make has to pass through the filter of God's Word. My only regret is that I waited so long to get started. Without wanting to sound preachy, today's children and youth need that for their own stability, well-being and mental and emotional health. I might also add that having a good church home—and a church family—is wonderful, especially when we have real struggles, like the loss of a loved one. They will be there for us.

Several years ago, a friend told me about an elderly, wealthy man who died in another city, and it was almost two weeks before anyone found him. That is really sad when you think about it, and he did not take any of his money with him. Here is a question that I would like to invite you to ponder: Would we be better off in America without religion? Answer this question and you will have insight: How many hospitals, universities, orphanages, and homeless and abuse shelters have been founded by the ACLU or the American Atheist Society? In case you missed it, the answer is none.

A human being consists of the body, mind and spirit. If we neglect the feeding of our spirit, it is like sitting on a two-legged stool or trying to win a fight with one hand tied behind our backs. The Word of God is powerful. Many times, when I am under a lot of stress and feel tension in my body, a few minutes of reading the Bible makes it go away. As the old American Express commercial says, "Don't leave home without it." I truly believe we should all live by this old admonition by an unknown author: "It is better to light one small candle than to curse the darkness." As a quick reminder, ***Your Future Begins Today***.

CHAPTER EIGHT
It's OK to Put Your Foot Down!

Several years ago, the Governor of our state dedicated a very large building in our community, saying, "This is the only building in the state of Arkansas where an airplane can take off and land and never leave the building." This is the kind of building it would take to hold all the books that have been written on the subject of dating and relationships with the opposite sex. Suffice it to say, I am not an authority on these topics, but they are very important for parents who are doing their best to prepare their children for happy, productive and successful lives. However, working with our schools and having children of my own has given me some valuable insights. I have also written a number of columns on these topics.

As a starting point, I would say the most important thing is to acknowledge that children are a special gift from God. It is the responsibility of parents to rear their children in a manner that will honor and glorify Him. Such practices will give parents the satisfaction of a job well done when children move out into the world on their own.

Rearing children is certainly not an exact science. Two or more children with the same parents can be as different as daylight and dark. I cannot count the number of times I have heard the voice of despair from parents of teenagers who have gotten into trouble, were failing in school, and were creating all kinds of problems for others and for themselves.

If you want proof of what I am saying, just go to a juvenile court sometime. You may have heard the saying, "Little children, headache; big children, heartache." Rearing successful children should be the goal of every parent and this is really the foundation for dating and relationships with the opposite sex.

I am sure you know that children today are much more mature at age 12 than they were at age 16 when I was growing up back in the 1950s. I may be old fashioned, but I believe that when a young girl reaches the age when she begins to date, a young man should come to the door and call on her, not sit out in the car and honk his horn. We should teach our children the importance of character and integrity, and as parents we should set the bar high and expect a lot from them. We usually get what we expect.

All children are different because they are unique. There is an important technique that parents should employ if they want to rear a well-mannered, respectful and successful child. We must not be too strict, we must not be too permissive, and above all, we must be the parents. When we are strict and impose boundaries, it says to the child that we love them and care enough to make sure they understand the difference between right and wrong. Again, this should begin early in life. Do not wait until he or she is a teenager to establish boundaries, as it's often too late by then. As I said earlier, times may have changed, but I see young adults every day who have great parents and have turned out to be wonderful human beings themselves.

We live in a time that has been called the sexual revolution, and unwanted pregnancies and couples living together outside of marriage are as common as a trip to the grocery store. In the beginning, I talked about the "law of cause and effect." These people are suffering the consequences of sin, living a life of unused potential and missing many of the greatest joys of life. They are missing out because no one cared enough or knew enough to teach them that there is a better way to live. It's really a matter of caring for others as much as we care about ourselves. A young man who has a deep respect for God's creation, the beauty of nature and the worth of a human being is not going to get a young lady pregnant out of wedlock. He understands that his selfish actions would severely limit this young lady's choices—as well as his own—for the rest of her life. Parents must establish rules for their children, including those dealing with curfews, touching, drugs, expectations for grades, etc.

Over the past several years I have gotten to know a wonderful human being by the name of Dale Brown, former basketball coach of the Louisiana State University Tigers in Baton Rouge. Sometime back I wrote a column about Dale—really about the influence his mother and others had on him when he was growing up in Minot, North Dakota. His father left his mother two days before he was born and his mother had to go on welfare to feed them. He said on two different occasions he saw his mother put on her heavy coat in the dead of winter and take 40 cents and 25 cents back to the store because the clerk had given her too much change. Over the next few years, Dale would become an outstanding athlete and set basketball records in his state that still stand today.

In the Catholic high school he attended, Dale was the "big man on campus." One day he was late for an appointment with the principal, who was also his coach. The penalty was that he would not be able to make the out-of-town trip that night to play another school in basketball. How could the coach do that to his star player? Dale learned a valuable lesson—one that parents should teach their children if they wish for them to have a sense of responsibility that will go a long way in helping them develop into an outstanding citizen. We should all long to preserve the innocence of youth, as seen in this quote by American clergyman and editor Lyman Abbott, "A child is a beam of sunlight from the Infinite and Eternal with possibilities of virtue and vice, but as yet unstained." P.S. If you have children of this age, it's OK to put your foot down.

CHAPTER NINE
Goals Are Vital to Achieve Success!

In 1956, Earl Nightingale wrote and recorded an inspirational message called "The Strangest Secret." This cassette recording went on to become the first message of its kind to sell a million copies.

I suspect that many readers have heard, or heard about, "The Strangest Secret." It is simply this: "We become what we think about." While Earl was the first person to write an inspirational message and record it with his golden radio voice, other great thinkers and philosophers have come to the same conclusion. Marcus Aurelius, who was a Roman Emperor, said, "A man's life is what his thoughts have made of it." Ralph Waldo Emerson said, "A man is what he thinks about all day long." Others throughout history have pretty much concluded the same thing.

Why am I sharing this with you? Because if a person thinks about nothing, he becomes nothing, and this simple truth illustrates the reason why it's important to have personal goals. A goal is something we would like to have or to be. It has been said that "a goal is a dream with a deadline."

It can be tangible (something we can see or touch) or intangible (something that that gives us personal satisfaction). Further, we need short-term goals as well, and we need goals for different areas of our life. Would you believe that research has discovered that only five percent of all working people in our nation have specific goals written down on paper? If 95 percent of working people who have no specific written goals had been taught the importance of setting financial goals when they were younger, many of them would not be facing the desperate economic conditions they are in today.

At this point, allow me to share Earl Nightingale's definition of success: "The progressive realization of a worthy goal." Now, please think about that for a moment. This means that any person who will take the time to decide what he or she wants to achieve and progressively work toward achieving it is a successful person.

That sounds simple, but only one out of every 20 working people makes this deliberate choice. The rest just leave it to chance and realize years later that chance does not work. The reason it's important to write goals down on paper is because each visual repetition drives the goals deeper into your subconscious mind. Now back to the question: when is the best time for a young person to start setting goals and to write them down on paper? I would suggest around 10 years of age would be a good time. Parents and teachers should remember that young people must be taught to do this and not leave it to chance. At this age they can have simple goals like making the honor roll, making the team, reading one book of interest outside of school, limiting television viewing to no more than three hours per week, taking an educational field trip at least once each month, and many others.

As the child gets older, goals will change to reflect his or her values and interests. The human mind was never meant to be a vacuum. However, without goals and worthwhile thinking, a mind is left open to every negative and impure thought that comes along. We do become what we think about.

As youngsters become teenagers and young adults, the influence of parents on their lives becomes less and less. They eventually leave the nest to move out into the world to have an independent life of their own. If they have been taught to set goals early in life—and to write them down on paper—the odds are pretty good they will continue. We are creatures of habit, which can be good or bad depending on the quality of habits formed. This is especially true when we discover how this process works.

Short-term goals take a year or less to achieve and long-term goals take longer than a year. Once a major or long-term goal is established, then a series of short-term goals may be necessary to help achieve it. Quite often, long-term goals can become foreboding and very discouraging because they seem so far away. Our short-term goals can work to give us that lift, or sense of fulfillment, that keeps us moving in the right direction. As I stated earlier, we need goals for different areas of our life and this is where I need to be more specific. As human beings we each possess an intrinsic quality called the self-governing factor, which is to say we would never seriously consider setting specific goals for our lives unless it were possible to achieve them.

The most valuable and productive goals are those which are specific as to time and degree. For instance, a business can set a goal to make a profit, but that is too vague to measure progress. A better goal would be to achieve a return of 10 percent on invested capital during the fiscal year 2020." Now that is a measurable goal. "To read my Bible more" is too vague, but "to read one book of the Bible each week for one year," is specific as to time and degree.

The following goals are only intended to be thought starters. Each of us must develop our own list of goals based on what is important to us. We should write them down on paper, since this simple act will make them much easier to attain because we can refer to them often. We should separate our goals into a short-term list and plan our day to make it productive, and we should also look at our long-term list every few weeks to make sure we are headed in the right direction. Later in the book I will share "The $25,000 Idea" that will be very helpful in this process.

Spiritual Goals

1. To become a member of a church, synagogue, or other spiritual organization of like-minded believers.
2. To develop a closer relationship with God by _____ (try to be specific here).
3. To read the Bible or Torah in full once each year.
4. To attend a Bible seminar or conference at least once each year.
5. To form the self-disciplined habit of daily Bible reading and prayer time.
6. To increase giving to my church or synagogue, and if not already, become a tither.
7. To attend my church or synagogue on a regular basis (again be specific: weekly, for instance)
8. To not be a C.E.O. when it comes to church. (Christmas & Easter Only)

Family Goals

1. To attend church or synagogue together as a family. *(This is especially important when children are in their formative years.)*

2. To have meals together with the whole family in attendance whenever possible. *(Make this a priority and turn off the television set and all cell phones.)*

3. To take trips as a family or go on vacations together annually. Make plans for interesting, educational and fun things to do.

4. To have a hobby or other activities where father/son—mother/daughter and vice versa—can interact together.

5. To allow children to have their friends over from time to time and make their guests feel welcome and special. *(Their friends seeing your family bond could make a difference in their lives. Keep in mind the parents must be in charge. Do it in the right spirit and your children will respect you for it.)*

6. To take time as a family to attend cultural events, plays, concerts, and live performances. Expose your children to some of the finer things in life.

7. To make grandparents a part of our family activities (if possible) since the family circle should include them as well.

School & Education Goals

1. To read good books to my preschool children on a regular basis. *(This will help prepare them to enter school)* To listen to older children read to you.
2. To respect my parents' rules because I know they love me and are doing their best to prepare me for the challenges that are ahead of me.
3. To work to excel and make excellent grades in all my classes in order to earn scholarships, since this may be the only way I can afford to attend college.
4. To be my own person, to set my own goals and not become a part of the crowd. After all, these people will not pay my bills.
5. To hold a family council from time to time to discuss and monitor the labor market, so I will be preparing for a career or job where I can find employment when I graduate. (I won't be like the young man who had a B.A., M.A. and a PhD. but did not have a J.O.B.)
6. To see the lifestyle of drugs and alcohol for what it is—one that limits my potential to become an outstanding person in my chosen field or career.
7. To understand that education is more than books and a classroom.

8. To seek out good mentors who will advise me and help me get a start in a career that has real potential for growth, success and personal fulfillment.

Work & Career Goals

1. To resolve that I will be an honest, dependable employee who works hard to help my employer succeed.
2. To understand fully, if I am employed in the private sector, that my employer must earn a profit to be able to give me a raise or a promotion.
3. To continually foster a positive attitude and be a good role model for other employees, especially for those who are newer on the job.
4. To understand there is no "I" in team and the best way to succeed is when we all pull together to provide better service for the customer.
5. To continually learn other facets of the employer or company I work for so that I will be in a position for promotion, more income and greater responsibility as the opportunities come along.

6. To understand, if I am employed in the public sector—teacher, coach, city, county, state or federal employee—that the taxpayers are paying my salary and retirement benefits.
7. To make self-improvement a lifestyle, taking special courses and training that will keep me from becoming outdated as new technology continues to change the work place.
8. To seek out and join trade associations and civic clubs in keeping with my career goals.

Income Goals

1. To understand that there are two forms of income. One is tangible, things I can see or touch; the other is intangible, things I can't see or touch but are nevertheless very important.
2. To understand the only job where I can start at the top is digging a grave. It's not where I start that counts, it's where I end up that really matters.
3. To understand that my income will be in direct proportion to my service and contribution. If I want more, all I have to do is increase my service to my employer or the one who pays my salary.

4. To avoid the credit card trap. These companies make it so easy to go into debt by spending more money than I am earning. Sooner or later, the payments come due. The school of experience may be a good teacher but the tuition is prohibitive.

5. To learn from my mistakes and avoid making the same ones over and over again. How to earn and save a portion of my income is a goal worthy of any person, young or old.

6. To look for ways to avoid digging myself into a financial hole from college tuition and other debts, if at all possible. The key to financial success has always been to spend less than I earn.

7. To apply the power of compound interest discussed elsewhere in this book.

Health & Physical Goals

1. To maintain a weight and fitness level that is normal for my gender and height. Habits to bring this about should begin early in life. One of our nation's biggest health problems today is obesity.

2. To have a doctor examine me early in life and recommend a diet and exercise program that will give me a proper balance

between fruits, vegetables, protein and carbohydrates.

3. To be conscientious in meal planning to ensure a balanced diet that will help me and my family live a healthy lifestyle.
4. To understand that a daily intake of foods high in fat, cholesterol and sugar increases the chances of a stroke or heart attack later in life. Most soft drinks are loaded with sugar. Drink water—lots of it—instead.
5. To do some reading on my own to learn what foods are best for me and which ones are not. In other words, to take responsibility for my own wellbeing.
6. To understand that germs are easily spread by human contact and to form the habit of washing my hands with soap at appropriate times during the day. This is most important after using the bathroom.

To live a long, healthy, productive life that is a credit to my parents, my teachers, and others, is a worthy goal for any person. As it has been said, "When you have your health, you have just about everything. "After we have taken the time to set our own personal goals, and have them written down on paper, the question then becomes, "How am I going to achieve them?" It took me many years to learn this, but once I have my goals established, I have learned that I need help from a higher power. There are two verses in the Bible that have really helped me. They can be found in Proverbs 3:5-6: "Trust in the Lord with all your heart and lean not on your own understanding. In all your ways acknowledge Him, and He will direct your paths." However, as I have said before, the reason most people do not succeed, even if they have goals, is that they quit too soon. It might be worthwhile to share a famous poem by an unknown author titled "Don't Quit." This poem has helped me over the hump several times.

"Don't Quit"

When things go wrong, as they sometimes will.
When the road you're trudging seems all uphill.
When the funds are low and the debts seem high,
and you want to smile but you have to sigh.
Rest if you must.
(But Don't You Quit.)
Life is queer with its twists and turns
As every one of us sometimes learns,
And many a failure turns about—
They might have won had they stuck it out.
Don't give up though the pace seems slow,
You may succeed with another blow,

Success is a failure turned inside out,
The silver tint of the clouds no doubt,
And you may be near when it seems far,
So stick to the fight when you are hardest hit.
It's when things seem worst that you mustn't quit."

CHAPTER TEN
Hard Work Pays Off!

There is an old saying that goes, "Give a man a fish and you feed him for a day; but if you teach him how to fish you feed him for life." There is contained within this old saying two key words that will go a long way toward rearing successful children. These two words are "give" and "teach." When parents truly understand that it is not wise to give their children everything they want without them having to earn it, they are on the road to rearing successful children who will make them proud after they leave home and move out into the world. More about this in a moment, but the teaching role of parents should begin soon after the child is born and not wait until he or she enters school. Also, parents should not depend on school teachers to teach children everything they need to know to be successful human beings. Children are born with natural instincts—to cry when hungry, the need to be changed when messy, and the desire for human touch and affection, for instance. As children grow older and become toddlers, they begin to develop their own unique personalities, and they also begin to test the limits of what parents will and will not let them do. Again, this is not a section about parenting, but about learning. When parents take the time to learn what works and what does not work, the chances for rearing a successful human being are greatly increased. We have all been around children who are polite, well-mannered, show respect for others and are eager to be helpful. These are traits we admire not only in children but also in adults, and you can bet these personal qualities were taught to these individuals, because they certainly didn't come as standard equipment at birth. Teaching others to become successful people brings rewards in proportion to the amount of time and effort put into the endeavor. The late John Wooden, the most successful basketball coach of all time, never called himself a coach, but rather referred to himself as a teacher. He taught his players the fundamentals—teamwork and a winning attitude—that can only come from achieving success and from winning. This resulted in 10 NCAA National Championships, a record that has yet to be equaled. What I have been talking about is building a strong foundation for a child's success. This is not easy in a world where his or her peers may have much more in the way of material things. This is why it is important to always maintain open communication with our children so that we are not only the parent, but also the child's friend. By example, we must help our children develop a strong work ethic. In the early days of our nation's history, fully 95 percent of Americans worked on a farm or in some agricultural industry. When a child was reared on a farm, there were constant chores to do, so developing a strong work ethic was natural. Many of our most successful people came from this kind of agrarian background. As time passed, our nation moved from an agricultural society to an industrial society. As mechanized machinery was invented and developed, millions of people moved from the farm to cities to work in factories that turned out products of various kinds. Still, the work ethic was fairly intact in our country. Even though most people no longer had to work from daylight to dark just to earn enough to get by, many children still had chores to do.

Then came the age of technology with the computer and other informational processing tools, and the burden of hard physical work was moved to other countries where cheap labor was available. It was then that most people no longer had to work hard physically to earn enough to get by, and obesity became a major concern. Next came the age of information where we are now, with cell phones, social media, YouTube, and all the rest consuming the time, energy, money, and creativity of millions of America's youth. Obviously, our nation's work ethic has suffered, and a child born into today's society faces a level of peer pressure that was not around in the days of our agricultural, industrial, and technological societies. The major problem, as I see it, is that we have several generations of parents who were not around in the days of a strong physical work ethic and have never experienced the values and rewards that older people understood from personal experience. Many people reading this book understand what I have been talking about, but many others do not. Regardless of our age or the era that we grew up in, a strong work ethic is still a thing to be prized when it comes to achieving happiness, success, and personal fulfillment. **This is the goal of this book.** Again, as I said earlier, it all comes back to what a child is taught when young and creating habits. I am a strong believer in working hard, but I also believe in working smart. We see people all around us who work very hard but do not achieve any real measure of financial success. On the other hand, we see those who work hard and everything they touch turns to gold. A lot of this has to do with setting goals. A strong work ethic is necessary to achieve outstanding success, but in most cases it's a matter of perspective. It's like the three men who were laying stones. When asked what they were doing, the first man said, "I am laying stones." The second man said, "I am making $10 an hour." The third man said, "I am building a cathedral." Same work, but they each saw what they were doing differently.

And so it is when building a successful human life. A child who grows up to become an outstanding success—something all parents desire for their children—learns many of life's lessons the hard way and does not complain when life deals a bad hand. Such children learn to be grateful for what they have been given and for the opportunity to succeed. The bottom line for what I have been saying can be summed up by this quote from English author P.G. Hamerton: "A strong life is like a ship of war. It has its place in the fleet and can share in its strength and discipline, but it can go forth alone to the solitude of the infinite sea."

The
Career, Lifestyle
&
Financial
Success
Years

From Age 30 to Age 65

Anyone who loves to eat watermelon knows that the "heart" of the melon is always the best, and it's also the sweetest. This is where we are as we continue our journey through *"Your Future Begins Today."*

We have now arrived at what could aptly be called the prime of life, where unless you are a professional student, your formal education is complete. You've likely also made decisions about marriage, career, where to live, and the line of work you wish to pursue. At this point, in the right kind of way, you should be serious about making your mark in the world—to be successful and to leave a legacy that you can be proud to own.

In a sense, this is like the days, however brief, when I was chopping cotton. If we are going to make progress, we have to spend most of our time in the middle of the field and not at the end of the row. If you will think about it, age 30 to 65 should be the most productive time of your life, and my heartfelt desire is to share ideas and information that is pertinent, timely and helpful. My goal is for you to glean from the following pages what would otherwise take you a tremendous amount of time and money to obtain from other sources.

A quick glance at the table of contents will give you a quick overview of the topics we will explore. Keep in mind that these are things I have learned along the way from 50 years of practical experience—50 years spent producing a daily radio program and a nationally syndicated newspaper column, making 1,700 speeches, writing 10 books (including this one, and founding an all-volunteer literacy project to help preschool children from low-income families. These are the children most likely to drop out of school, have difficulty succeeding, and cause problems for all of us in society. One thing you can believe, I want the very best for you and count it as a real privilege to share these ideas and concepts with you.

However, what I have just shared comes with a warning label that needs to be said: we can be the smartest person in the world and still fail if we don't use what we know. As an example, I know people who have gone to college and completed more than 300 hours of course work, yet they still don't have a degree or a plan. These people do not want to face the real world or try to get a job, so they just stay in school, which is easy if someone else is paying for it. The topics I have selected were written for the individual who is out of high school or college and is beginning the quest for success in the world of work, from which most of our rewards come.

When we know who we are and where we are going, it is so much easier to succeed in a job or career, and also in life. Self-confidence and a healthy self-image come from working, succeeding and saving a portion of our income. When we take the time each day to develop a mental or written checklist, and make it as productive as we possibly can, the days add up to a successful week, month, year and lifetime. It's true—the world will step aside for the man or woman who knows where they are going.

CHAPTER ONE
Law and Order Reign Supreme!

When I was a kid growing up in a small town in southeast Arkansas, we had a saying in reference to the local authorities in our community. We would say, "That man over there is the police, the other man is the sheriff, but that state trooper—he's the law!"

We are a nation of laws, the outflow of a duly representative democratic government, for which we can all be grateful. Our system of government and law beats anything else on earth, hands down. The law has not always been applied even-handedly, but it is still the law. It is the heart of man—not the law—that is wicked, and this compels man to take unfair advantage of his fellow man. The villains here are most often greed and the thirst for power, prestige and material possessions, which are the natural effects of a sinful nature. The truth is, we may avoid the laws of man for a while but there are greater laws that can never be broken. With respect to my getting involved with our legal system and breaking and violating our laws, I will confess that I have lived a very dull life, and I hope it continues. To the glory of God, I have never been arrested, never been in jail, and never been subject to a sobriety test. As I have gotten older and matured, I've continued to obey the law, but for a different reason. For most of my life I obeyed the law out of fear that I would be caught, but today I obey the law because I respect and appreciate our system, and am grateful for the opportunity just to be an American—to live and work in the greatest country in the world. Let me be quick to add that I am certainly not perfect in respect to obeying the law. I can remember getting three traffic tickets in my life: one for speeding, one for not coming to a complete stop at a traffic sign, and the last for cutting through a service station one night to avoid a stop sign. I also got a citation one time from the Game and Fish Commission for having one fish over the legal limit.

This last citation happened when my former business partner, the late Bob Gannaway, and I took his grandson Randy on a trout fishing trip on the beautiful White River in north Arkansas. The trout limit was six for each person and Randy, being underage, did not have to have a license. We were catching a lot of trout and I knew we were getting close to the limit. About this time, a game warden pulled alongside our boat. He got into our boat and counted our catch. Would you believe we had 19 trout, one over the legal limit of 18? I tried to take the blame so only one of us would get a ticket, so I said, "I caught that extra trout." Randy said, "Did not." Since Bob and I both had a license, we both got a ticket. Even though that was more than 50 years ago, I still remember it. That ticket cost each of us $28, and back then $28 was a lot of money, at least for us. Now, let me change gears for a moment. What I have just shared is about as simple and elemental as you can get. Every day, the media, and especially our newspapers, are filled with descriptions of all kinds of lawsuits, judgements and violations from the local to the state and federal governments. These acts violate local, state and federal laws, and some even violate international law that impacts the United States and her citizens. I am well aware of the large number of high-profile people in America today who have broken the law and dominate cable news for days and weeks on end. One of these was Bernie Madoff, who took unfair advantage of investors with his elaborate Ponzi scheme. Is it really worth it to go through all that embarrassment for family members and others who are also affected by their crimes (not to mention the problems associated with you going to prison)? More than 10 years ago, Bernie Madoff's oldest son committed suicide. While the wheels of justice sometimes grind very slowly, in the vast majority of cases our legal system works. And even when it doesn't, those who are never caught still have to live with themselves. We have all heard the saying, "what goes around comes around." Sadly, the people who willfully break and violate the law are simply an accident waiting to happen. My message here is simple. Just go back and reread the chapter "Don't Shoot Yourself in the Foot" and you will have a better understanding of this great principle that always works. The Bible says it another way, "As ye sow, so shall ye reap." What I am saying is not about these lawbreakers— it's about you and me. If we have had good parents or good mentors who have given us sound value systems (to be honest, to tell the truth, to respect the rights and property of others), we will obey the law because it's the right thing to do, regardless of what path others may choose. Here is something that former President Harry Truman once said that adds credibility to what I have been saying: "The basis for our Bill of Rights comes from the teachings of Exodus and St. Matthew, from Isaiah and St. Paul. I don't think we can emphasize that strongly enough these days. If we don't have a proper founded moral background, we will finally end up with a government which does not believe in rights for anybody except the state."

CHAPTER TWO
Facts Change But Principles Do Not!

If you have ever heard the beautiful song by Ray Boltz titled "The Anchor Holds," you will have a good mental picture of a concept that makes all the difference in the world in terms of achieving success. Sadly, there are so many people in our society today who do not have an anchor, and they are adrift in the sea of humanity, being buffeted by every wind or tide that comes along. If you happen to be this person, or know someone like this who lacks direction or purpose in life, then take heart: I have some good news for you. Several weeks ago, I finished reading a fantastic book titled, *"The 7 Habits of Highly Effective People"* by Stephen Covey. If you have not read this book, I highly recommend it. I have always considered myself to be a fairly stable, well-adjusted person, but I learned a lot of things from Dr. Covey's book that I never knew or thought about before. One point in his book that has stuck with me is where he talks about how we get our sense of value and self-worth. He lists a number of centers where this takes place in the lives of different individuals. For example, if our personal value and self-worth come from being centered on our spouse, family, work, money, possessions, self, church, friends or any number of other things, when we encounter a serious problem with any of the people or things on that list, we fall apart. Our emotions play a vital role in our stability, and when they are fractured or strained, this can have a serious and adverse effect on us. On the other hand, he says that when we are principle-centered, and our value and self-worth are tied to principles, we are then free to take action or respond in a manner that is best for that particular circumstance. Principles don't react to anything. They don't get mad or treat us differently. They won't divorce us or run away with our best friend. They aren't out to get us. They can't pave our way with shortcuts or quick fixes. They don't depend on the behavior of others, the environment, or the current fad for their validity. Principles don't die. They aren't here one day and gone the next. Even more importantly, we can be secure in the knowledge that we can validate them in our own lives, by our own experiences. There is something else that I have observed that may be helpful to some people who will read this book. Sometimes very handsome men and beautiful women are at the greatest disadvantage. This is particularly true for women. From the time they are beautiful little girls, the world shows them favoritism—from winning beauty pageants, to having their photographs appear in highly flattering places, and later to having men line up on the highway to fix their flat tire. Such favoritism includes having all kinds of doors opened, just because of their beauty. This also carries over to employment, as they are definitely favored here as well. In a nutshell, this is how beautiful people relate to the world. If they don't take the time and make the effort to get highly qualified, apart from being handsome or beautiful, they are often in a world of hurt once they get older and their beauty fades, as it often does. This problem is exacerbated, especially for women, if she goes through one or more divorces. Again, it all comes back to what Dr. Covey was saying about living a principle-centered life. If we will take the time and make the effort to learn about principles and how they work, this will be the best insurance we can have for old age. To be successful and happy, it all boils down to treating others like we want to be treated, and to be honest, dependable, trustworthy, kind, loving and efficient. Such a person is someone others love to be around. When we work to become qualified and earn our own success, it makes all the difference in the world. As American political leader William Jennings Bryan once said, "Destiny is a matter of choice: it is not a thing to be waited for, it is a thing to be achieved."

CHAPTER THREE
True Wealth Is Not Money!

It has been said that the American Free Enterprise System is the Eighth Wonder of the World, and the average American's lack of understanding of what it is and how it works is the Ninth Wonder of the World.

Without question, this marvelous economic system has given the American people more prosperity, more success stories, and a higher standard of living than any other system in the history of civilization. However, like owning a car and never changing the oil, in recent years our Free Enterprise System has become sluggish and is not performing anywhere near its true potential. This is before President Trump came along. You may say, "If this is true, why should I care?" Since your future and the future of your children and grandchildren, if you have any, will be impacted by decisions that are being made by our leaders and policy makers, it might be profitable to spend a little time thinking and learning about our nation's economic system.

It should be noted from the beginning that
"true wealth" is not money or material possessions.
It is about lives, freedom, health, families and
relationships, and is ultimately about our relationship
with our Creator. With that said, our nation's
economic system does impact each of our lives,
and as noted, we call our system the American Free
Enterprise System.

First, what is the American Free Enterprise
System? It is the free flow of goods and services
from manufacturers and producers to consumers
without undue government laws, regulations, and
policies. The motive for manufacturers, producers,
and service providers is to earn a profit, and the
goal for all of these people is to be able to keep a
percentage of the profit for themselves to improve
their standard of living. Really, it's an incentive
system. You kill the incentive—the goose that
lays the golden eggs—and you essentially kill the
system.

We call those involved in this form of
commerce the private sector, meaning they have
private ownership. Our government at three levels—
local, state, and federal—taxes this business activity
to pay the salaries and other expenses of those who
manage and regulate the system known as the public
sector. The public sector means that all the assets
controlled by the government are owned by every

tax-paying citizen in our nation. Those who work for the government are called public-sector employees. It should be noted that public-sector employees pay taxes, too, in the form of income taxes, sales taxes and many others. To facilitate transactions, when people purchase goods or services, we have something called money or currency. In the old days, and still used by some, this was done by barter—that is, the trading of goods and services for other goods and services. But barter is cumbersome and money makes exchanges much easier. As mentioned earlier, some people think that money is wealth, but it is really a "medium of exchange" to move goods and services to the consumer. We can also stockpile money for use later to buy bigger and better things. The federal government makes monetary policy for our economic system and controls the printing and distribution of currency. This activity is coordinated by the Federal Reserve System. But who really knows how much money is needed in order for our nation's economy to keep running smoothly? Remember my earlier example of owning a car but never changing the oil? We hear the term "inflation" used all the time. But what is inflation? It is simply a rise in the general price level often caused by too many dollars chasing too few goods. When the government causes the creation of more money by taxing, printing or borrowing, and then a corresponding increase in production, the money you have in your pocket will purchase less.

Here is an example. To reduce it to the lowest common denominator, let's say the government, by its control of the money supply, causes spending to be $1,000 and there are only 1,000 items sold. What is the value of each item? One dollar, right? The government then increases the money supply and causes spending to increase another $1,000 without any increase in items sold. At this point, what is the average price of each item? Two dollars, right? Now, you get the picture. I remember when you could buy a soft drink for a nickel. In the earlier days of our nation's history, when our economy was much healthier, our government, in order to support itself, simply levied a tax on items that supposedly constituted "true wealth." This could be land, buildings, livestock, businesses, and anything else that was tangible. But as the country grew and expanded, the government grew right along with it. So did the number of government employees. Remember, these are "public" employees and they do not ordinarily produce anything that is tangible. One thing that makes our economy unhealthy is simply this: we have too many public-sector employees riding in the wagon and too few private-sector employees pulling it. This, along with several other factors (like excessive taxes and regulations), has caused many of our nation's manufacturers to move to other countries where labor rates are lower and tax rates are more favorable. Our nation's unions bear some responsibility here as well. When vast numbers of people are unemployed, they do not contribute to the system but rather they help to drain it like what happened in 2010 when unemployment benefits were extended for 99 weeks. What contributes to a healthy economy is a good balance between the private and public sectors.

Ever hear of a tax increase? When national politicians give away the store (to everyone in their district and elsewhere) in order to get reelected, they force the government to borrow money because they do not want to face voters who have just had a tax increase. After incurring a national debt of more than $20 trillion, we have dug a real hole for ourselves. Can we recover? Yes, if our elected representatives develop sound fiscal policies and take the necessary steps to repair the ship of state. Granted, this is not an easy subject to address, especially with limited space, but hopefully we will all try to become better informed. That is what I plan to do. A good place to start to begin to understand the meaning of true wealth, both tangible and intangible, is how it impacts our nation's economy and our lives.

CHAPTER FOUR
Reading Sharpens the Mind!

During our lifetimes we are exposed to all kinds of information. This process begins the day we are born and continues until the day we die. We first learn from our parents and others around us in our formative years. We learn from relatives, friends and neighbors. This process continues in school, then in college (if we attend), and then later in the real world, as we call it. As you read this book, you are simply getting more information that will form yet another layer on your subconscious mind where our information is stored for later use. This book is intended to give you good, reliable information and advice to help you improve your life, to succeed, and to be a happier person. It is intended to be informational and inspirational in nature.

While I would never presume that you would value this book so highly, it is my hope that you will view it as a constant life companion—something to be kept close at hand and read and re-read on a regular basis. There may be times, however, when it appears my thoughts and comments are somewhat

negative or harsh. But my unfailing motive is—
when taken in context—that this information will
benefit you and every other reader, especially when
it is considered over the long term.

Unlike many books that concentrate on one
specific subject and allow the author to go much
deeper, this book covers a wide range of topics that,
in one way or another, impact the lives of all readers.
If you consider what I have presented up to this
point, and will present in the pages to follow, there
are books available that will go as deep as you want
to go and give you insights far beyond these topics
where I have only scratched the surface. There are
hundreds of good books out there, but we should be
selective in what we read. We should stay clear of
trash because reading trash just creates baggage that
we don't need. Remember the G.I.G.O. principle—
Garbage In Garbage Out! Also, we should make
sure we are reading factual and truthful information.
As Will Rogers once said, "It's better to be ignorant
than to learn a lot of things that just ain't so." For
these reasons, I have included a "Recommended
Reading List" at the end of this chapter. This list
includes books that will help to bridge the gap
between where you are and where you would like to
be. As someone once said, "There is nothing in the
world that needs to be done that good books won't
help us to do better." Sadly, it took me many years

to finally figure this out. As a result, I have missed a good education that a lifetime of reading would have given me. However, over the past few years I have done a good job of making up for my deficiency. It is rewarding to be able to tell you that I have read each of the books on my list, plus many more. With all the technology available today, a lot of people are getting their information from the internet and other electronic devices. That's both good and bad. Granted, I am from the "old school" and have yet to see where all the social networking and other electronics are taking us. What I see now are many companies using the internet to make and market a plethora of products—and earning huge profits. I also see a lot of Americans wasting valuable time on these products that could be used to accomplish useful and worthwhile things that would help them have a successful career and life. When you think about it, the only thing we don't have more of is time. Once it's gone, it's gone forever. The key, of course, is balance—to do those things that are productive, but at the same time, to not waste untold hours that will produce nothing but a large phone bill. Because the younger generation is so much more in tune with— and efficient in —receiving electronic information, they say a day is coming when all of our information will come from these sources. Again, I may be old-fashioned but I remember a time when they said that everyone would use an ATM instead of a traditional bank, and tellers would become a thing of the past. That didn't happen. Why? Because people love and want the personal touch; a real live person meeting their needs. The newspaper industry in America is struggling today for several reasons, with one being that young people are not buying newspapers. They say they are getting all or most of their information from the internet or other sources that do not require hard-copy information. Each morning, I have a ritual. I go out and get the local newspaper, fix a pot of coffee, and then sit down with the newspaper in my hands and read it. The same is true for books. I have a great home library and cherish all the books that are just sitting there waiting for me to pick them up. I frequently go back and re-read some of the best ones. I give many books away, wanting to share them and their contents with other people. Here is the best case that I have ever discovered for reading books, especially the good ones that have life-changing information. Sometime back, former Arkansas Razorback football coach Ken Hatfield told me that to really get the message in a book, we have to read it seven times. As previously noted, repetition is the key to retain what we read because we don't really know anything if we can't remember it. To experience the joy of reading, if you don't already, why not set a goal to read at least one good book each month? This is a sensible approach and a good place to begin. Keep this up for an extended period of time and you will see the benefits of expanding your mind and your vocabulary. A mind that is stretched by a new idea can never again return to its original shape. A constant stream of new ideas can make a tremendous difference in our lives, and this will come about through a lifetime of reading. Don't use expense as an excuse not to read. That's what libraries are for. You already pay for them with your tax dollars, and most libraries these days also have audiobooks to listen to in your car. Then there are book clubs, e-books, used books, garage sales, used book stores, book review clubs, books on Amazon, etc. Try keeping two or three good books on your nightstand. Pick up and read from one, depending on your mood, every night before you turn out the light. You will be amazed at how much you'll learn, investing only 10 minutes or so a night. Turn off your television and Smartphone and simply read.

Recommended Reading List

I have personally read each of the following books and can highly recommend each to you. In turn, you can recommend them to those who look to you for advice and counsel. Regardless of the problems or challenges we face, a good book can provide a source of information that will make a wonderful positive difference in our lives.

1. The Holy Bible
2. The Tipping Point—Malcolm Gladwell
3. Outliers—Malcolm Gladwell
4. A Game Plan for Life—Coach John Wooden
5. Gifted Hands—Dr. Ben Carson
6. Same Kind of Different as Me—Ron Hall
7. See You at the Top—Zig Ziglar
8. The Strong-Willed Child—Dr. James Dobson
9. How to Win Friends and Influence People—Dale Carnegie
10. He Still Moves Stones—Max Lucado
11. John Adams—David McCullough
12. Word to Lift Your Spirits—Coach Dale Brown
13. Common Sense—Thomas Paine
14. People Who Live at the End of Dirt Roads—Lee Pitts
15. The Thread that Runs so True—Jesse Stuart
16. A Walk Across America—Peter Jenkins
17. The Greatest Salesman in the World—Og Mandino
18. Tough Times Never Last, But Tough People Do—Dr. Robert Schuler
19. Psycho Cybernetics—Dr. Maxwell Maltz

20. The Seven Habits of Highly Effective People—Dr. Stephen R. Covey
21. None of These Diseases—Dr. S.I. McMillen
23. Granny Camp—How to Bond With Your Grandchildren—Anne Dierks
24. Uncommon—Coach Tony Dungy
25. The Anti-Alzheimer's Prescription—Dr. Vincent Fortanasce
26. A Framework for Understanding Poverty—Dr. Ruby K. Payne
27. Battle Ready Moms Raising Battle Ready Kids—Reba Bowman
28. Don't Make a Budget—Ken Robinson

CHAPTER FIVE

Who is the Real Boss?

A while back, I was talking with a lady friend of mine who told me about a shopping trip she took to a major department store. She said that when she got ready to check out at the register, she was the only one in line while two female clerks were engaged in conversation. She went on to say, "I stood there for over a minute and neither clerk offered to check me out. At this point, I cleared my throat to let them know that I was there. With this, one of the clerks turned to me and said, 'Would you mind?,' indicating she would check me out when they finished their conversation." More about this in a moment.

First, I want to share another true story along the same lines but with a completely different attitude. There is an owner of a dress shop here in our community who uses a very simple concept to train her new salespeople. When the store is empty and the clerks are engaged in "busy" work, if the front door opens and a potential customer comes in, she will turn to her clerks and say in a low voice, "Don't look now, but your paycheck just came in the door."

Here is the bottom line and something every person in America needs to understand regardless of who pays their salary. In the American Free Enterprise System, the real boss—the one who pays the salary of every single person, either directly through profits or indirectly through taxes—is the customer. If we don't know and understand this, we are going to suffer financially for the rest of our lives, or at least until we are taught and wise up.

If you are in the age bracket from 30 to 65 years of age, or have children or grandchildren in this age range, and are self-employed or work for someone else, you also need to understand the role of the boss in our nation's economy and in society. If we are in the public sector, where our income comes from taxes, we still have a boss. Every person has a boss. In some cases we have many bosses, and we just need to understand who they are. As long as we are not doing something dishonest or illegal, this is where the law of cause and effect comes into play. We should serve others with the right attitude and give an honest day's work for an honest day's pay. In the long run, this is the only way to succeed and move up the ladder of success. Don't fall into the trap of trying to take shortcuts—in most cases they only lead to dead ends and, ultimately, failure.

Sometime back, I discovered the following in my files. I don't know the author, but it pretty well says it all:

"There has never been, there is not now, and there never will be any boss but the customer. He is the one boss we must please. Everything we own, he has paid for. He buys our home, our cars, and our clothes. He pays for our vacation and puts our children through school. He pays our doctor bills and writes every paycheck that we will ever receive. He will give us every promotion we will ever obtain during our lifetime and he will discharge us if we displease him."

Now, going back to the beginning of this chapter and my example of the two sales clerks, here is something I ran across titled "The Customer that contains real wisdom, something we should all be reminded of from time to time.

The Customer

The customer is the most important person in our business. The customer is not dependent on us, we are dependent on him. The customer is not an interruption of our work. He is the purpose of it. The customer does us a favor when he calls. We do not do him a favor by serving him. The customer is part of our business, not an outsider.

The customer is not someone to argue with or match wits with. The customer is the person who brings us his wants. It is our job to supply his wants. The customer deserves the most courteous and the most attentive treatment we can give him. The customer is the person who makes it possible to pay our salaries. The customer is the lifeblood of this and every other business."

Having said all that, in closing this chapter I would ask that you ponder this question: "Is the customer always right?" We have heard that all of our adult lives, and the answer—as we have read above—is Yes!

A friend of mine told me several years ago that at a luncheon meeting of advertising professionals he heard Herb Kelleher, the founder and then-chairman of Southwest Airlines, one of the best customer service companies in the world. Kelleher shocked the audience by telling them that the customer is *not* always right. But then he explained. He said that he would not tolerate a passenger on one of his flights being rude, vulgar, and unreasonable with one of his flight attendants or other employees. He would rather give them their money back and tell them to take their business— and rude behavior—to one of his competitors. He strongly believed in customers, but he also believed in supporting his own employees. So often there are exceptions to some rules. But the customer is USUALLY right, since they are THE BOSS.

"Business underlies everything in our national life, including our spiritual life. Witness ... in the Lord's Prayer; the first petition is for daily bread. No one can worship God or love their neighbor on an empty stomach."

—President Woodrow Wilson

CHAPTER SIX

A Man Paid $25,000 for an Idea!

The world runs on good ideas. Every product, every invention, every poem, every symphony, every anything known to man, at one time was just an idea in some person's mind. However, ideas are like slippery fish. If we don't gaff them with the point of a pencil and put them on paper, they may slip away and we can spend many months or years trying to recall them. (Amazingly, the subconscious mind usually will reproduce it eventually.)Fortunately for mankind, there is one idea that did not slip away, and it has been called "The $25,000 Idea." This idea has the great potential to help any person who is willing to learn what it is and then put it into practice. If you would like to get a lot more accomplished in the days ahead, this could very well be the idea that can make it happen for you. Several years ago, just by chance, I discovered this idea, and it has been one of the most practical and helpful ideas that I have ever used. Sometime after the turn of the last century, Ivy Lee, a consultant with the Rockefeller Foundation, was making a sales call on Charles Schwab, chairman of the board of the Bethlehem Steel Company.

Lee was telling Mr. Schwab that he could help him do a much better job of managing his company. Mr. Schwab broke in and said, "Look, what we need is not more knowing. What we need is more doing. If you can tell me how to get more done, I will listen and pay you what I think your ideas are worth." At this point, Ivy Lee asked Mr. Schwab to take a piece of paper and a pencil and write down the six most important things he had to do the following day. This took about 20 minutes.

When he completed this task, Lee told him to go back and number the six items in order of their importance. This took another 10 minutes. When he had finished, Ivy Lee told him to put the paper in his pocket to review before going to bed. Then, the first thing the next morning he was to go to work on number one, continue until number one was completed, then move on to number two and so forth, on down the list. If something should force his delay, go on to the next item. This way he would always be working on the most important tasks and in order of its importance. When each item on the list was completed, repeat the process. It should also be noted that by developing a new list each day, the most important tasks would always be first at hand.

In about six months, Mr. Schwab wrote Ivy Lee a letter and told him the idea he had given him was the most profitable that he had ever received, and he enclosed a check for $25,000. You can just imagine what that $25,000 would be worth today. It was later reported that the simple idea of writing down the six most important things to do each day, and numbering them in order of importance, was responsible for turning a little-known steel company into the second largest independent steel producer in the world. Now, here is another factor that, while it may not be obvious, is critical to the success of this idea. Before Mr. Schwab could write down the six most important things he had to do the following day and arrange them in the order of their priority, he had to first know what his goals were. This is what I was talking about in my previous discussion on goal setting.

What is truly exciting about this idea for me—and hopefully for you, too—is that it will work for any person regardless of age, gender, or station in life. When it comes to tasks around our home, my wife is great at making a list and then checking off one item at a time. She is truly organized and can get more done in a day than most folks can in a week. Granted, this is just a simple way to use this idea, as she is certainly not an executive with a large corporation. If you are not already doing this, give it a try. I bet you will be surprised at how much more you—and your team—can get done. And you don't even have to send me $25,000.

Now, here is an important point that I hope you won't miss. This idea can be used not just for small things but also for big things, like growing a business, setting up a retirement plan, planning a once-in-a-lifetime vacation, moving up the ladder in your job or career, and any number of other worthwhile goals you may have set for yourself. You probably are going to have to establish some shorter-term to-do lists as part of those bigger things. But the lists work, at every level.

Don't stop here, because there is a bonus that has helped me tremendously over many years. I employed this $25,000 idea back when I was in the printing business selling motivational programs and growing my base of radio stations and newspapers as a self-syndicated commentator and newspaper columnist. During this time, I was wise enough to systematically save some of my income, which lessened the financial strain today. Of course when it comes to real earnings, many people today are just getting started by the age of 50. If so, this is fantastic because you should be able to give back even more in the remaining years of your life.

Here is what I have discovered about setting and reaching goals—and it's a great way to keep from being frustrated when you don't reach them. Over the years, I have set many goals that I did not reach. After a while, there is a tendency to stop setting them. After becoming a committed Christian, my faith deepened and I have learned that I can trust God and turn my fortunes and my life over to Him. I have said many, many times, "God has a timetable." This way I don't have to fret or have any stress, because I know that things will work out for the best and for His glory in His time, so long as I do my part,. We still need to do our part—to write our goals down on paper, but it's His timetable that will make a difference.

CHAPTER SEVEN
Be Careful Who You Learn From!

As a young printing salesman in Little Rock, Arkansas, back in the late 1960s, I had the good fortune of working for a man by the name of Bert Parke, who was president of a printing company and was very active in the community. I had spent the previous seven years with another printer working in production. Because I had learned a good deal about the business and had inherited my father's gift of gab, Bert took a liking to me. Of course, it did not hurt that I was selling a lot of printing and earning his company a good deal of money. Over the next several months, I became active in the Little Rock Chamber of Commerce and the United Way, and even was elected to the Pulaski County Quorum Court, where I served on the Budget Committee.

Back in those days, the Little Rock Chamber of Commerce went on an annual "good will" tour to other cities, where we were hosted by their chamber members. We were given the red-carpet treatment, meeting community leaders, learning a good deal about their city's history and economy, and picking up some great ideas that we could take back home. During the years I worked for Bert, we went to San Antonio, Houston and Denver. Each of these trips was great, and for a young 30-year-old, I received an invaluable education I still benefit from every day. The first year, we went to San Antonio, where they were opening the Hemisphere, a World's Fair–type event. At one of our meetings I was in the same room with former Texas Gov. John Connally as he was taping some television spots to promote the grand opening.

The following year, the trip to Houston was just as exciting. I had the privilege of meeting then-Mayor Louie Welch, and touring the newly opened Astrodome, which housed Judge Roy Hofheinz's quarters. I also got an inside look at NASA and took a trip on the Houston Ship Channel, where many imports enter the United States. The last and final trip was made to Denver, Colorado. There were countless highlights on this trip, including a visit to the Loveland Ski School, where I never quite mastered the technique. I found out one thing: when you point those ski tips downhill, you had better to be ready to go. We stayed in the Brown Palace Hotel, and my room was on about the 15th floor looking down on the gold dome of the Colorado State Capitol. I had met Gov. John Love at a reception the second evening we were there.

As a quick aside, something happened on that trip that I will never forget. One evening at about 9 p.m., a member of the staff of the Little Rock Chamber invited me to go down to the bar on the bottom floor and have a drink. While I am not a drinker, and never have been, I went along just for the chance to spend some time with him. Soon after we arrived, a lady came up to me (I found out later they were called "bar flies") and asked me to buy her a drink. I was caught off guard and so I said, "I can't do that because I am a preacher," which was not the truth, of course. Well, the next morning at the big breakfast, with more than 400 people in the room, they started the program and paused for the invocation. Who do you think they called on to do this? It served me right. As I said earlier, this is something I will never forget and hopefully I have learned a lot of important things since those days.

You may be wondering why I have taken the time to share these personal experiences with you. On this trip, I learned one of the most valuable lessons that anyone could ever learn in terms of achieving success. I want to pass along these lessons, and I hope they will be of value to you.

I learned that the most important and successful people on these goodwill tours, and that's who we had from the Little Rock business community, were also the nicest people you would ever meet. I learned that these people would help you if you needed help. Rather than going out on the town with some of the others on these trips, I preferred to sit around the hotel lobby and just visit with many of these men. I really got to know them. Remember, I was a 30-year-old young man from a modest family, who had dropped out of college a few years earlier.

There is an old saying that every man puts his britches on the same way—one leg at a time—and this is certainly true. However, on these trips I learned to be comfortable around top executives and was never again intimidated at the thought of making a sales call to any of them. This insight may have also helped me in my speaking career, as getting up before a large audience was much easier knowing that those in the audience, regardless of their status, were just people. And the nicest people were those at the top. While thinking about this chapter a few days ago, I recalled several people who have been mentors to me. A "mentor" is a wise and trusted teacher or guide.

These names won't mean anything to you because, in all likelihood, you probably won't know them. But I hope you will seek out good mentors who will help you along the way. They will help you if you ask them and are worthy of their help. Now, every person may not need a handout, but I am talking about a hand-***up*** to help us have a successful job or career. First, there was Bob Gannaway, my business partner for over a decade and my former Dale Carnegie instructor. And there was Ed Riddick, a highly successful engineer who helped me in many ways, especially later in selling the Earl Nightingale programs.

Here is one other quick experience that will demonstrate the ways of top people. One of my printing accounts was Wright, Lindsay & Jennings law firm in Little Rock. The office manager, Millie, and I became good friends, and by then I had learned the value of having some good mentors. Well, Ed Wright just happened to be the President of the American Bar Association at that time. I told Millie that I would like to meet Mr. Wright and that I would like to learn from him. She not only made this possible but arranged for us to have lunch at the Capitol Club, which was on the top floor of a bank building, the second tallest building in the city.

When I arrived for our luncheon appointment, Mr. Wright greeted me, and while he did not eat a bite, he carried my plate for me as we went through the food line. We had a wonderful visit and the experience was priceless. This man, who had reached the pinnacle of his profession, was humble and gracious. These are qualities that will help any of us to be happier, more successful, and fulfilled as a person. I have found that more often than not, people who have "arrived" and are successful will welcome the opportunity to help younger people on their way up. Many of them remember people who helped them in their own careers and want to pass it on. So, seek out potential mentors and ask. Of all the answers they can give, only one is "no."

All of this to say very simply, be careful from whom you learn. People with a good heart will always be willing to help us. As I have said so often before, *Your Future Begins Today*.

CHAPTER EIGHT

Watch Out for Dishonest People!

My father was considerably older than my mother. Because of this, he had been around several years longer than my mother when I was born. He was wise to the ways of the world and he had made a lot of mistakes, but he had learned from them. He told me that he had bought enough whiskey to float a battleship, but when I was born, he swore off of it. I never saw him take a drink in the 40-plus years that I knew him. As a result of his influence, I have never taken a drink of any kind of alcohol in my life. To be sure, I have done things much worse, but thankfully, I have been spared the pain and heartache that comes to so many people in our nation who live with an alcoholic or who have been impacted in a negative way. I can't even imagine the pain that comes to so many families who have lost loved ones because of a drunk driver.

A lot of people these days are into genealogy. When my father told me that he left Kentucky in 1919, running from the grand jury for shooting craps on a Sunday, I never had much desire to research the family tree. I was content to let sleeping dogs lie. In his obituary, his occupation was listed as farmer and restaurant owner, but earlier in his life he had a most unusual occupation. His nickname was "Cowboy" because he rode a horse out in the country and would buy livestock, mostly cattle. He would then drive them to a rail-head, ride with them on a train to the cattle yards in Kansas City, sell them for a profit, and return home. He really taught me something when he told me that occasionally he would run across someone he could not trade with. He said, "Don't make them mad. Just go on down the road and you will find someone that you can trade with."

While I did not realize it at the time, he had a great impact on my value system because he spent many hours telling me what was right and what was wrong. He was not a religious person, never went to church, but he came from an era where a man's word was his bond and all it took was a handshake to seal the deal. What he taught me back then has stayed with me all these many years. One of the things I learned is to stay away from dishonest and unethical people. I had a chance many times to use this knowledge when I was selling printing in downtown Little Rock, and later in other areas of life as well. As an outside salesman, you do have some discretion as to the people you call on in terms of new prospects. As a human being, we are creatures who have feelings. If I made a sales call to someone for the first time and I got the feeling that they were dishonest or unethical, I just did not go back and call on them again. Usually their off-color language gave them away.

There is an old saying that goes, "Birds of a feather flock together." This is true. As a general rule we will seek out people, in and outside our work and especially in our social life, who make us feel comfortable. If we have high standards, these are the kinds of people we want to be around. Of course, the reverse is also true. What I am going to say next may be a long-stretch, but most of what I have been saying is directly related to literacy. The people in this world who are completely illiterate not only miss opportunities for personal success but also live by the law of the jungle. Getting the right kind of education is really the key to success, and we can't get that until we learn to read. This should help to explain why I am so passionate about our all-volunteer bookcase literacy project. When these people become highly proficient in reading, they can pass this on to their children and grandchildren.

I would like to close this chapter on a high note with a quote from Napoleon Hill, author of the best-selling book, ***Think and Grow Rich***." Hill said: "If you are successful, remember that somewhere, sometime, someone gave you a lift,

107

an idea that started you in the right direction. Remember also that you are indebted to God and others until you help some less fortunate person just as you were helped."

CHAPTER NINE
Stress Can Kill You!

The story goes that a man went to the doctor one day and asked him to give him the secret to living a long life. The doctor said, "What you should do is put a little gun powder on your oatmeal each day. That should do it." Well, this man took the doctor's advice and it worked. He lived to be 93 years of age, outlived three wives, left behind eight kids, 27 grandkids, and a nine-foot hole in the crematory wall.

I hope you at least cracked a smile as you read this, or maybe even laughed out loud because laughter is good for what ails us. It's also a good way to avoid or relieve stress, something that takes a toll on millions of people in our nation today. It has been reported by many reliable sources that more than 50 percent of all patients in hospitals today are there because of psychosomatic reasons, which is to say, emotional effects on the body with special reference to certain disorders.

One of these disorders is stress, which means emotional or intellectual strain or tension. While we all have stressful times, for the sake of our overall health it's better to not have periods of prolonged stress if we can avoid it. Stress is a modern-day phenomenon, something we have seen increase with our fast-paced lifestyles. Our forefathers did not have much stress for the simple reason that they worked it off. If you have done much hard physical work for 10 to 12 hours a day, you know what it's like to go to sleep the moment your head hits the pillow. Because of modern technology, most people in America do not work that hard physically any more. However, untold millions of people are working longer hours for a variety of reasons. I think this may be the reason for the saying, "You can burn the candle at both ends, and it does produce a brilliant flame, but it sure is hard on the candle."

This condition is responsible for the modern-day phenomenon we call "burnout." Have you ever been involved in a job or project and worked so long and so hard that you burned out? As it relates to this, I heard a story a while back about a school teacher named Maxine. She went to her principal and said, "I've had it up to here. I'm stressed out. The other teachers don't like me. I can't get my kids to mind and I am burned out." The principal said, "Maxine, before you can get burned out, first you have to be lit."

Another story tells of a woman who came into the bedroom one morning and said, "Johnny, it's time to get up. School starts in an hour." Johnny answered, "But I don't want to go to school today." "Why not?," the woman asked. "Because the students don't like me, the teachers yell at me, and I'm stressed all the time. Tell me why I have to go." The woman answered, "Because everyone expects you to be there, and because you are the principal."

I will confess that over the years I have had a good deal of stress for a variety of reasons. A good part of the reason was my lifestyle, working long hours, not eating the right foods, and not getting enough of the right kind of exercise.

Eating fried potatoes and greasy steaks prepared on the grill, especially in my younger years finally took a toll, and this practice clogged up my arteries. It resulted in a triple heart bypass about 40 years ago. They say these things last about 10 to 12 years, and they were right. About 15 years ago, I had my second triple bypass, and even though I am now past 80 years of age, this really got my attention. Today I work out on a regular basis and watch my weight a lot more closely. This all came about due to stress. You would not believe the number of food labels I have read in the past few years as I monitor the fat, cholesterol, salt and sugar content of each food choice. Even though you may be between 30 and 65 years of age, a couple of good questions to ask yourself are, "Am I under a lot of stress?" and "Can I see health problems down the road if I don't change my lifestyle?"

Sometime back, "Small Business America," a newsletter of the National Association for the Self-Employed, listed 10 causes for burnout. If you have any inclination that you may be headed for burnout, assuming that you are not already there, you might want to think seriously about these causes to see if one or more relate to you.

- Do you feel yourself under pressure to succeed all the time?
- Do you need to generate excitement again and again to keep from feeling bored?
- Is one area of your life disproportionately important to you?
- Do you feel a lack of intimacy with the people around you?
- Are you unable to relax?
- Are you inflexible once you have taken a stand on something?
- Do you identify so closely with your activities that if they fall apart you do, too?
- Are you always worried about preserving your image?
- Are you taking yourself too seriously?
- Are your goals unclear, shifting back and forth between long-range and immediate?

Anger is another great cause for stress. While I have never had a problem with anger, a lot of people do. Think about those who have road rage. If you or someone you love has a problem with anger, I recommend a terrific book titled, *"None of These Diseases,"* by Dr. S. I. McMillen. In his book he has two important chapters: "It's Not What You Eat—It's What's Eating You," and "The High Cost of Getting Even." These two chapters alone are worth the cost of the book many times over.

Go back and reread the earlier chapter, "Reading Sharpens the Mind." It will make all the difference in the world if you are not already an avid reader. However, it's not just the fact that we read, it's what we read that makes the biggest difference. We should read for pleasure but we should also read for profit and good information that will help us to be happier, more successful, and fulfilled human beings. Your future really does begin today.

CHAPTER TEN
Learn to Love Yourself!

One of my relatives has told me many times that she suffers from low self-esteem. Because I don't walk around in her skin, I don't know all the reasons for this malady, but I do know that millions of Americans suffer this same fate each day of their lives. If you suffer from low self-esteem, hopefully I can help you change your values and your perspective.

First, what is self-esteem? It is simply the opinion you have of yourself, or the way you feel about yourself. It's a little bit different than self-image, which is the mental picture we have of ourselves, but they are closely connected. While the opinion we have of ourselves has been around since a savage hurled an insult instead of a spear, the self-esteem movement actually started back in 1969 when psychologist Nathaniel Brandon published a highly acclaimed paper called "The Psychology of Self-Esteem." He argued that "feelings of self-esteem were the key to success in life," and his idea soon became the new thing in education. At the apex of this craze, the California Legislature even established a self-esteem task force for the state's schools.

But here is the problem with teaching self-esteem: It doesn't work. Writing in the Wall Street Journal about 15,000 studies the movement generated, reviewer Kay Hymowitz concluded: "And what do they show? That self-esteem doesn't improve grades, reduce anti-social behavior, and deter alcohol drinking or anything good for kids. In fact, telling kids how smart they are can be counterproductive. Many children who are convinced they are little geniuses tend not to put much effort into their work. Others are troubled by the latent anxiety of adults who feel it necessary to praise them constantly."

In time, we read the headlines: "The Death of the Self-Esteem Movement." Good riddance. Now, that's the academic side. Allow me to now get down to the practical side and some common sense. What many people don't know or won't acknowledge is that we are each created in the image of God. When we can understand and believe that we were created in the image of an all-loving, all-wise, and all-powerful God, we will view ourselves and others in a way that we never have before. At this point, we come to realize that we have all the worth and value that we are ever going to have—all we will ever need. Now, what value we make of ourselves and what value we are to others and to society are different stories. For the most part, this is left to each one of us.

Here is something that I have had tucked in my files that will give you additional insight into what I mean. It is titled, "What's Your Worth?" Just think about this for a moment: "A small bar of iron is worth about $5 to start with, but made into horseshoes, this same bar of iron is worth about $10.50. Made into screwdrivers, it may be worth about $250. Made into needles, this same bar could be worth about $3,250. Made into balance springs for watches, its worth could go up to $250,000. The same thing is true for another kind of material—YOU! Your value is measured by what you make of yourself. This is why people go to school, take self-improvement courses, read good books, and chart a course for their own personal development.

Here is a thought I had earlier while thinking about writing this chapter. You can't have a good or healthy self-image if you do bad things. Our mind's eye sees everything we do. The Bible says we can't get both sweet water and bitter water out of the same tap. To develop and sustain a good self-esteem is a lifelong process. When we do things right, honest and true, we develop over a long period of time a good opinion of ourselves, and we feel good about doing something productive rather than saying positive phrases that have a short shelf-life. When we do bad things, all we have to do is ask God—and those we have wronged —- to forgive us and then learn from our mistakes. We all make them and we should not constantly beat up on ourselves, as this distorts the true picture of worth and value we have as human beings.

Former President Harry Truman once said, "I studied the lives of great men and famous women, and found that the men and women who got to the top were those who did the jobs they had at hand with everything they had of energy, enthusiasm and hard work." And I might add, that is exactly what it takes to build healthy self-esteem. The great news is that it is never too late to start for most people.

If we suffer from low self-esteem, we can begin right where we are to place our life and future on a solid foundation. This takes place when we live a life of doing good and right things, as this will produce dividends far beyond our greatest expectations. It is a little late for those who have a terminal illness or who have been sentenced to life in prison. But even in such cases there is something people can do to make things right with God, if they feel the need. He loves and cares for them right to the very end.

The Retirement Community Service & Legacy Years

From Age 65 to the End of Life

The legendary Yogi Berra, baseball Hall of Fame catcher for the New York Yankees, is also famous for his witty sayings known as "Yogi-isms." One of my favorites is, "When you come to a fork in the road, take it." Well, Yogi, I am pleased to say that the fork we are taking is the one that leads down the home stretch. We have looked at the "Toddler, Teenage & Young Adult Years," and the "Career, Life-

119

style & Financial Success Years," and now we will explore topics that focus more on the "Retirement, Community Service & Legacy Years." Of course, many people are really at the heart of their career when they reach 65 years of age. You may know that the fastest growing age group in our nation is the centenarians. This is to say 100 young.

One good example—and there are hundreds— is Col. Harland Sanders, founder of the Kentucky Fried Chicken empire. While he had worked as a cook in several restaurants in his earlier life, he did not start his KFC enterprise until he was 65 years of age, and he used $105 of his first Social Security check to call on potential franchise owners to get started. As I said a moment ago, many people do not do their best work until they are in their 60s, 70s and even 80s. This is especially true for people who are creative and do not require a lot of physical strength to continue their productive lives.

With that said, for most people the die is pretty well cast by age 60, and they are either financially successful or on the road to financial success. Of course, financial success is only one indicator of true success. While the title of this book is *"Your Future Begins Today",* and this is true for each of us—all along the path of life, there are challenges and opportunities that should give us a great deal of happiness and personal satisfaction. For me personally, an average person who loves people and has worked hard during my 50-year career, my greatest satisfaction has come in my later years with my involvement in projects that give back to my fellow man. As you read this, if you are 65 years or older, you will relate to the following chapters in a very real way, as you will be living the things I talk about. If you are a younger person, these are things for you to know for the future and to think about as you go through life.

As I conclude this special time with you, here are some end-of-life issues that I need to share. There is one thing for sure: we are all going to die. And it just makes sense that we should make arrangements and provisions for our final expenses before we reach that time. We should have a burial plot or crematory picked out and, if possible, paid for. We should make arrangements for our own funeral: how it will be conducted, and who will be involved. Above all, we should have made peace with God and established where we will spend eternity. Beyond these basic things, we should make plans for the eventuality that we may develop a terminal illness that could play out over several, weeks, months, or years. Do we have the resources to pay for a long-term care facility or will we be able to stay in our own home, where most people would rather be when they die?

While this is personal and may not interest you at all, I want to share something for you to think about. I have said many times that I don't know how people make it without having a church family. If something should happen to me, I have no doubt that members of our church family, especially members of our Sunday school class, would be there to take care of my wife Janis. My own family would help, but they are all so far away that it would be impractical to count on them. As the Boy Scout motto says, it is just my nature to "Be Prepared." In America, we have so much to be thankful for and I am just grateful that I was born in this great nation.

CHAPTER ONE
A Better Society Begins With Me!

Have you ever given any thought as to what obligations, if any, you have to society? The word "obligation" means "the duty, promise, contract, etc., by which one is bound." Based on this definition, we all have a variety of obligations to parents who brought us into this world, teachers who educated us and gave us the chance to succeed, spouses to whom we made marriage vows, children we brought into the world, employers who gave us a job or sanctioned a career, and countless others. But beyond these personal relationships, do we have any obligation to society or the larger body of humanity with which we share space, especially as it relates to our country?

In other words, do you feel any obligation to go beyond just taking from our system, and making some worthwhile contribution to the success and welfare of those involved in personal relationships, especially when it comes to giving back? Do you feel an obligation to produce more than you consume? You are a literate person, and as you read these words, I am sure you are already contributing and giving back and will appreciate this reminder of some basic things you may have forgotten.

The American political and economic system is based on the opportunity and success of the individual citizen and not on any particular group of people (no matter what the political parties say). However, if we are to be successful, happy, well-adjusted and productive human beings, there are certain fundamental concepts that we must know, understand and obey. The most important of these concepts can be seen when people are called to be a witness or testify in a jury trial. Before they are to give sworn testimony, an official of the court will ask them to raise their right hand and answer the following question: "Do you swear to tell the truth, the whole truth, and nothing but the truth, so help you God?"

Of course, the answer to this question is always "yes." Whether they truly do or not is a matter of conscience, and is between them and God. Of course, there are penalties for those who do not tell the truth. This concept is basic to our legal system and to our way of life. Here is something that may not be common knowledge. The United States of America may be the only nation in the world which claims, as our heritage, that our government gets its authority and power from Almighty God. All the other nations seem to derive their authority and power from some other source such as a monarch, military leader, or political party.

To confirm what I am saying, listen to these words from the Declaration of Independence: "We hold these truths to be self-evident, that all men are created equal, that they are endowed by their Creator with certain unalienable rights that among these are life, liberty and the pursuit of happiness." Notice this statement says "Creator," and that is God. That's why a person in our legal system who is sworn to tell the truth does so by stating "So help me God." What I have told you here is just background information, but it is necessary to understand the basic bedrock principles that govern the American economic and political system.

When individuals reach legal age, they are no longer subject to the rules and regulations of parents. They are free to make their own decisions and incur legal obligations for which they are responsible. When people sign a car note or home mortgage, or really any other contract, they are obligated to pay it back. If they don't have sufficient net worth, usually they have to have a co-signer or someone else who will be responsible if they cannot make payments in a timely manner. Really, a successful life is all about obligations, whether it's obeying the law or making sound moral and ethical decisions and all of us are held accountable.

After we become legally accountable for our personal decisions, it then becomes our obligation to help those who are following in our footsteps, since they will be the leaders and producers in our society for future generations of Americans. When we reach the end of our days on this earth, if we have been successful and have lived a good, honest and productive life, those who have given us opportunities will be more than rewarded for the faith and trust they have placed in us. When I reach the end of my days, I just want God to say: "Well done, good and faithful servant." (Matthew 25:21) It is still true, *Your Future Begins Today!*

CHAPTER TWO
An Investment in the Future!

In any discussion about how individuals can find a way to give back, it should be noted that we don't have to be retired or have a lot of money to do so. Any person who has a job, is healthy, and who appreciates what others have done for them can give back in a variety of ways. It should also be noted that there are millions of people in our country who give back every day, just because of the job or career they have selected. Among this group you will find teachers, police officers, firefighters, nurses and those serving in our nation's armed forces that put their lives on the line to preserve our freedom. Of course, there are many others too numerous to mention. You might say, "Aren't these people just doing their job and getting paid for it?" Maybe so, but they also chose that job because they were conscious of the need to serve others.

Here is a story one of my readers sent to me some time ago that will answer this question far better than I ever could.

One time, a company CEO was at a dinner party, and he decided to explain the problem with

Jim Davidson

education. He argued, "What's a kid going to learn from someone who decided his best option in life was to become a teacher?" He reminded the other guests of the old saying, "Those who can, do ... and those who can't, teach." To emphasize his point, he said to one of the guests, "You're a teacher Bonnie. Be honest, what do you make?"

Bonnie, who had a reputation for frankness replied, "You want to know what I make? Well, I make kids work harder than they ever thought they could. I make a C+ student feel like one who has just been given a Congressional Medal of Honor. I make kids sit through 40 minutes of class time when their parents can't make them sit for five minutes without an iPod, video game or movie rental. You want to know what I make? She paused again and looked at each and every person at the table.) "I make kids wonder. I make them question. I make them apologize and mean it. I make them have respect and take responsibility for their actions. I teach them to write and then I make them write. Keyboarding isn't everything. I make them read, read, read. I make them show all their work in math."

"They use their God-given brain—not the man-made calculator. I make my students from other countries learn everything in English while preserving their unique cultural identity." She

continued, "I make my classroom a place where all my students feel safe. I make my students stand, place their hand over their heart and say the Pledge of Allegiance to our flag, one nation under God, because we live in the United States of America. I make them understand that if they use the gifts they were given, work hard, and follow their hearts, they can succeed in life."

Bonnie paused one last time and then continued, "Then when people try to judge me by what I make, with my knowing that money isn't everything, I can hold my head up high and pay no attention. You want to know what I make? I MAKE A DIFFERENCE. What do you make, Mr. CEO?"

His jaw dropped and he went silent. Other people in the room applauded.

Here is probably the most valid point of all. I just bet that all the people on the list of careers I mentioned earlier also give back in many other ways. You want to know why? It's because they have a good heart and love other people, and while they have to pay their bills like everyone else, their priorities are different because they are called to serve.

I am reminded of the slogan that has made the email rounds several times: "If you are reading this, thank a teacher. If you are reading this in English, thank a soldier." Both are in the people-serving business. Giving back is something that should come naturally for people who are truly blessed, and it should be taught to children while they are still very young. Many times I have rung the bells for the Salvation Army in our community, and it's truly a blessing to see parents teaching their children to give back by placing money in the kettles.

There is absolutely no limit to the ways we can give back. All we have to have is the desire. We see financial giants like Bill Gates and Warren Buffett give away billions of dollars to charity through their respective foundations. We see organizations like the PGA, the NFL, and the NBA give back as a whole, along with many of their individual players. We also see movie stars and celebrities, who make big money, give back in many ways. All of this helps.

While this is wonderful, it pales in comparison to the vast number of people giving back at the local level in their communities. There are people every day who work at hospitals, soup kitchens, food pantries, homeless shelters, literacy projects, churches and synagogues, civic and service clubs, and countless other places. Many of these people are recognized for their good work and caring spirit, and are all deserving. The Bible says, "It is more blessed to give than receive." (Acts 20:35), and I personally know this is true. There are basically two kinds of people in this world who have resources and good health: the givers and the takers. It is left up to each of us to decide which group we are going to be in. As you read this, I hope that you choose to be a giver and, as we give together, that our giving back will help the less fortunate. We can inspire them to want to do better, because someday they will want to give back, too.

Another important area where we can give back is to take an active role in helping to conserve our natural resources. One of my favorite slogans (and T-shirts) reads: "EARTH: Don't throw it all away." Of course, this refers to recycling, but it can also refer to so much more of all of us. As citizens of the world, we have an obligation to be good stewards of what God has created, to educate ourselves and to rear our families to be green-minded.

CHAPTER THREE

One Lives and Gives, the Other Dies!

Former English Prime Minister William E. Gladstone once said, "Selfishness is the greatest curse of the human race." The reason his statement is true is because of human nature. It is just natural to look out for number one, to grab, to push or shove, and to make sure our own needs are met first. This is also true for the animal world. Did you ever see two dogs sharing a bone?

The irony of this human failing is that the person who is selfish is also the one who loses in the end. I am reminded of the man in the Bible who pulled down his barns to build bigger ones for storing his crops and goods. The Lord said, "Thou fool, this very night thy soul will be required of thee." (Luke 12:20)

To my way of thinking, there are only two ways to overcome the curse of selfishness. The first is love, in particular to love other people enough that we are willing to put their needs above our own. It is easy for most parents to love their children enough to do this. And husbands and wives also have, in most cases, the love to do this for each other. To go beyond this requires a kind of "brotherly" love that we see exhibited by many people in our society. However, there is a vast difference between the person who gives to others from his surplus and the one who gives sacrificially.

The second way to overcome selfishness is to believe and understand the law of cause and effect that I talked about earlier in this book. This law controls everything in the universe, and it basically means that for every action there is a reaction. If we want more, we have to give more. Over time, we always get back from others what we first give to others. It is important to understand that we don't always get back from the ones we gave to, but we must get back from someone because that is the way this law works. Another way to say it is that we can't out-give God, because He keeps the score.

Here is another example to help us see more clearly how this natural law or principle works. Several years ago, I was privileged to serve as chairman of the Speakers Bureau of the Pulaski County (Little Rock, Arkansas) United Way. I learned the following story called "The Tale of Two Seas."

If you go to a world map and locate the land that is now called Israel, you will see that the Jordan River flows into the Sea of Galilee, and continues for 83 miles before flowing into the saltwater lake known as the Dead Sea. The Dead Sea has no outlet and the surface of the sea is 1,292 feet below sea level, lower in elevation than any other place on earth. It contains no animal life and the surrounding area is almost a wilderness. It is one of the most saline lakes in the world.

I am told that it's impossible for a person to sink in this body of water. Come to think of it, I have never heard of anyone drowning in the Dead Sea. The principle illustrated by "The Tale of Two Seas" is simply this: the Sea of Galilee has fish and an abundance of marine life. The Jordan River passes through this body of water, so it both receives and then gives. It also lives. At the other end of the Jordan River, as it enters the Dead Sea, it receives but it does not give. And it dies.

In a very real sense, this is also what happens to us as human beings. A human being can give without loving, but we cannot love without giving. We would all do well to remember, "The service we render is the rent we pay for the space we occupy." There is nothing on earth more satisfying than to be able to give back to those who really need our help, especially when we can provide a hand-up and not a hand-out. And just remember, *"Your Future Still Begins Today."*

CHAPTER FOUR
They Are Spending Our Money!

Former President Franklin D. Roosevelt once said, "Any government, like any family, can spend a little more than it earns, but you and I know that continuance of that habit means the poor house."

President Roosevelt is no longer with us, but I think he would be appalled at what is happening in our nation today. We have been on a spending binge for many years, and this has placed our nation so far in debt that we may never recover, at least in my lifetime. Since our elected officials are in charge of the public treasury, it would behoove all of us as private, taxpaying citizens to hold our elected officials accountable for the way they spend our money.

The vast majority of our elected officials are honest, trustworthy and conscientious when it comes to discharging their duties. But unfortunately, many are not. In the case of these individuals, we would never want to leave the "fox to guard the henhouse," and this is why we must be even more diligent going forward to get involved in public affairs and to know what is really going on. What I am saying here is not in any way meant to be partisan. Ever since I started my weekly newspaper column back in 1995, I have been most careful not to endorse any political party or candidate for office. I have friends, both on the state and local levels, who belong to both of our major political parties, and I am sure some of them have been annoyed with me because I would not serve on their committees or attend various political functions.

To say it as simply as I know how, I want what is best for America and her long-term future. This is not about politics; rather, it is about my concern for our children and grandchildren and what kind of life they will have in the years to come. When our elected officials betray the sacred trust they are given when they are elected and sworn into office, we should boot them out of office the next election. I have strong views when it comes to making laws and national policy, as these determine everything in terms of spending and the size of our government. For example, the number of government employees has grown exponentially over the past two or three decades. When you have politicians argue that "stimulus" is the answer because it will put people to work, there is a point that is mostly overlooked.

When we add employees to the public payroll, the money to pay them has to come from an appropriation (local, state or federal), and that appropriated money will come to an end at a specified period of time. This means they have to appropriate more money if they are to continue to be employed and paid. On the other hand, when you create jobs in the private sector business and industry, where employees are paid from profits, those jobs continue year after year and they do not require any appropriation from the public treasury. For some, this may be difficult to see, but over the long term this is in the best interest of our nation's financial stability. This means a better, more stable economy which helps every wage earner in America, both public and private. In the past few years we have gotten back many jobs that went overseas when conditions were not favorable for them to stay.

It should be the goal of all Americans to become better informed about issues that directly impact their lives. Most illiterate people are not well informed—probably not informed at all! When we are responsible citizens who are better informed, it is much easier to elect public officials who have our interest and America's interest at heart, and therefore will make decisions that will put us back on solid financial footing. This is why it is in our national interest to hold our public officials accountable. As the famous Irish philosopher and playwright George Bernard Shaw once said, "Action is the only road to knowledge." We owe it to future generations of Americans. To be sure, they are spending our money.

CHAPTER FIVE

Freedom Will Always Precede Opportunity!

Former President Dwight D. Eisenhower once said, "Freedom from fear, injustice and oppression will be ours only in the measure that men who value such freedom are ready to sustain its possession—to defend it from every thrust from within or without." If you are at least 65 years of age, you can remember a much simpler time in our nation when we were truly free. We were free in so many ways the younger generation would find hard to believe. We were free to walk the streets anywhere in America—even at night—without fear of being mugged. We were free to leave our doors unlocked, our keys in the car's ignition, and even to correct someone else's children without fear of being sued; and we had countless other such freedoms.

Obviously, something has happened in America over the past 70-plus years to change that simple way of life that my generation cherished back then. One of the things that really made a difference was that we studied American history and knew the price our forefathers paid for our freedom.

I just finished reading again the classic *"Common Sense"* by Thomas Paine. It has given me greater insights and appreciation for the freedom so many of our younger generations take for granted. They were not around during the Revolutionary War when we won our independence from England, or during World Wars I and II, when everything we were and had was on the line.

If we had lost either of those wars, we might be speaking German or Japanese today. But thank God for the brave men and women who served in our Armed Forces and fought and died so we could remain free. Now there is another threat to our freedom that is much more subtle and dangerous than we as a people have ever faced before. This threat is that of radical Islam, with 1.5 billion people who have sworn to take over the world and impose Sharia law on every human being on the planet.

What I am going to share in this chapter is not done because I am a vindictive person, but rather one who has some common sense. No American or true patriot should ever forget what happened to our country on September 11, 2001, when Muslim Al Qaida terrorists flew two airplanes, loaded with passengers into both World Trade Center towers in New York City, taking the lives of more than 3,000 innocent people. Two other planes were hijacked, one crashing into the Pentagon in Washington, D.C., and the other crashing in a field in Pennsylvania after brave passengers took it over and kept it from its intended target. To be sure, our nation is at war with radical Islam. It should be noted that not all Muslims are radical or terrorists. The vast majority are peace loving. However, it is estimated that 15 to 20 percent are radical enough to strap a bomb to their bodies in order to kill Christians and Jews. If that number is correct, it means that there are around 300 million Muslims out there ready to take you and me down.

The sad thing is that the majority of Americans do not take the threat of radical Islam seriously. In fact, the Pew Research Center, an independent, non-partisan, public opinion research organization, tells us that United States citizens are essentially oblivious to the potential danger of radical Muslims. According to recently released poll results, 58 percent of Americans said they knew either "not very much" or "nothing" about the Muslim religion, Islam, which is the fastest growing religion in America.

Sometime back, there was a documentary shown on Islamic television in which young children sang of their desire to participate in violent jihad or to become suicide bombers. The program went on to show never-before-aired footage from a radical

Islamic rally in California, where the audience was told, "One day you will see the flag of Islam over the White House." All you have to do is try to board an airplane these days and you will have a better understanding of what I am saying.

As a humorous aside, sometime back I saw a cartoon with a plump, older woman standing in front of an airline ticket counter, and she said to the agent, "Oh, I'm not flying anywhere. I am just here for the pat down."

I just want my fellow Americans to think about what I am saying because freedom is the most precious thing we have. We should always keep in mind that freedom is vital and will always precede opportunity. Our leaders and policy makers are making choices that will definitely affect our lives.

CHAPTER SIX
Every Human Being is Important!

The English critic and essayist William Hazlitt had it right when he said, "Prejudice is the child of ignorance." The word prejudice, according to the dictionary, means, "A judgment or opinion formed before the facts are known: especially an unfavorable, irrational opinion." It also means hatred of, or dislike for, a particular group, race, religion etc.

We see many forms of prejudice in the world today. Here in our own country, prejudice tears at the very fabric of who we are as a people. One of the most obvious forms of prejudice is people who are looked down upon because they were not born with handsome features or outstanding beauty.

Every once in a while I get to thinking that there is something wrong with me. You see, I like to kiss frogs. Now, before you turn me off completely, let me tell you what I mean by this. The "frog" in this case is someone who was not blessed with good or even average looks and may even be what we call ugly or homely. Frogs could also include those people who are shabbily dressed, perhaps lack good self-esteem and maybe the resources to do better. Please understand, I am not talking about the top executive who leaves home for a quick trip to the grocery store without bothering to put on a suit and tie. People with high self-esteem carry themselves in a different way. They are easy to spot because they have self-confidence.

It is also important to note that I am not talking about physically kissing someone. Rather, I just look them in the eye with an acknowledgement that they are a human being, and give them a friendly smile or maybe a cheerful greeting. It has been said that we should treat every person as though their heart were breaking, because it very well could be. When I am out in public—at the bank, the grocery store, the post office, or anywhere my travels take me—I encounter these people all the time. If they will make eye contact, which is not always the case, I will speak to them and acknowledge them as a person.

In terms of your own success, what I am saying may be much more helpful to you than you realize. If you have any doubts about the value of acknowledging people, hopefully you will come to the correct conclusion before I am finished. Based on what I have shared, here is a little experiment that I would like to invite you to do the next time you are out in public. When you come across an extremely handsome or beautiful person, take notice as to how they will most time look you straight in the eye, smile, and greet you in a positive way. On the other hand, notice how those who are not as traditionally attractive will many times not speak or make eye contact with you. I believe the latter comes as a result of many years of rejection by people who are prejudiced or have their values in the wrong place. Make no mistake, being rejected is painful. I believe it's even more important to make these people feel special because they are.

Let me make sure we are on the same page. When I talk about the fine art of kissing frogs, I am not talking about just being friendly, since anyone can do that. I am talking about seeing someone who really needs a lift and going out of our way to give it to them. Now, here is a word of caution. As I said, there is a fine art when it comes to kissing frogs. We don't ever do it if these acts could be misconstrued or suggestive in any way. There is also a question of culture. Many women who have come to our country from Eastern cultures will not look a man, other than her husband, in the eye because of the rules of the society in which she grew up.

To be sure, race relations would certainly be better if everyone took time to acknowledge other people and make them feel special. A lot depends on whether or not we are prejudiced. All we have to do is stop and realize that every single person is created in the image of God and that every person has value and worth, even those who are the "frogs" in our society. I am always amazed at those people who want to get ahead in their job or career, or to earn more money or a promotion but never understand that their attitude and personality are going to count much more than all the knowledge and expertise they could ever acquire.

Because we are each different and unique, this simple technique of kissing frogs may not appeal to you. However, this is a win-win situation. When we can do this successfully, everyone is a winner and it does not cost a penny to put this concept into practice. Once you do, I believe you will keep doing it. Regardless of your age, gender, or the job or career you may have, we are all in the "people" business. To be genuine and to have a desire to help and serve others are the best ways I have discovered to succeed in whatever we may be doing. Here is a truth that goes all the way to the core—Every Human Being is Important!

CHAPTER SEVEN
What Will They Say About Us?

The word "legacy" is an interesting one in the English language. It means, according to the dictionary, "Anything received from or passed on by an ancestor, predecessor, or earlier era."

In view of this definition, here is a simple question that we would all do well to think about—What kind of legacy will we pass on to future generations of Americans? To me, this is a sobering question because what we will be leaving our children and grandchildren may not be that great, what with a nation riddled in debt, crime, poverty, high unemployment, and corruption among our elected officials. This has served to shake the confidence of even the most optimistic among us. As I write these words, this is only a snapshot of where we are as a nation at this time, but the story does not end there. This is what gives me hope and a reason to press on.

There are a number of reasons why our generation may be the first to leave our children and grandchildren with fewer expectations for a better future than we inherited from the previous generation. Why is this true? Again, a plethora of reasons, but I believe it all started at the end of World War II when people had more money to spend, and before what I feel was the breakdown of the home and the traditional American family. Before the days of high inflation and high expectations that caused both parents to have to work, we had fewer material possessions but more character, which is the bedrock of our society. This was reflected in our nation's educational system. Fifty years ago, the United States of America led the world in test scores for reading, math and science. Today, studies show that we rank 18th out of 21 industrialized nations in these important benchmarks.

If we are to rebuild our country and restore the tarnished American dream, we must do a much better job of educating our youth. This will require a return to traditional family values, where parents spend more time with their children and academic education is a top priority in the home. Personally, I believe one of the greatest threats we face is the proliferation of the giant tech companies who are spending billions of dollars on advertising to hook kids on electronic devices that waste untold hours of their time. Insecure kids, whose parents don't spend quality time with them to teach them real values, are like sheets blowing in the wind and are not preparing themselves for a successful life.

The world's—and our nation's—greatest enemy has always been ignorance. To the degree that we allow this despot to control our lives, we will sink deeper into the abyss and dig the hole even deeper than it already is. Only through reading, study, and the application of life-changing principles can we hope to have a brighter future. That is really the essence of what this book is all about. It is to help all readers to discover and use more of their God-given potential, and to work together in preparing our nation's young people for the important years ahead. All throughout history, the nations that have been subjugated by others are those with high rates of illiteracy. Our very freedom depends on an informed and enlightened electorate.

I love to work with children. They are bright, optimistic, and are like sponges when it comes to absorbing new information. As parents, teachers and society in general, let's make sure it's the right kind of information that will prepare them for the days when they will leave the nest. Get them started reading early, take them to the library, buy them good books, let them see you reading, and make academic education a top priority in your home. My priority has always been academics first, with sports and other activities somewhere down the line.

149

Jim Davidson

Here is a quote by former President Grover Cleveland that we would all do well to think about: "And let us not trust in human effort alone, but humbly acknowledge the power and goodness of Almighty God, who presides over the destiny of nations, and who has at all times been revealed in our country's history, let us invoke His aid, and His blessing upon our labors."

And here is a thought to consider for the rest of our lives—yours and mine. What kind of legacy will we personally leave for family and friends to recall when our name comes up? Will the person who performs our funeral have some true and good things to say? Our LEGACY matters because it is evidence of a life lived over a finite period of time here on this earth. I want mine to be good and I am sure you do, too.

The Miracle of Compound Interest!

W hen the Pandemic came to our shores in March 2020, I dare say no one knew the devastation it would wreak in the lives of millions of Americans. The lives that would be touched and the thousands of precious souls who would die from COVID-19, as it came to be called, are a matter of record. This issue was addressed at the beginning of the book, but there is a connection to a heartbreaking story that has touched me deeply. This was to see the long lines of people waiting to get food because they had nothing to eat. The reason they did not have food is because they had no money. Just think about that—in the most prosperous nation on earth, there are thousands of people, perhaps millions, who are not able to afford even the most basic of necessities.

This is a sad condition, in spite of the fact that in 1964 President Lyndon Johnson launched his War on Poverty, in response to a poverty rate of around 19 percent. Today, more than 100 million Americans are on some kind of poverty relief program, and if the long lines of people wanting and needing food are any indication, we have lost the war. Back when I was growing up we did not have any government giveaway programs, but rather every adult had something called "saving for a rainy day." It worked pretty well, as I cannot remember anyone going hungry and there were not "panhandlers" on every busy traffic corner, as we have here in my community.

The best insurance against poverty is something we call a "savings plan," and for those who get started early in life, there is the "Miracle of Compound Interest." This miracle not only insures against poverty, but almost guarantees wealth for the individual who is wise enough to start saving early in life. The following chart shows how it works. Take note of what happens to the growth rate in later years, especially the 15 years between years 25 and 40. But more about this a bit later. This information was provided by my good friend Dr. Ben McNew, a former bank examiner and professor at several major universities.

To get a visual of the power of compound interest, consider how much money would be in our account if we saved a fixed amount each day or week and invested it at the end of the year. The following chart shows what one, two and five dollars a day saved would be worth in so many years, if the interest rate was 10.5 percent and if compounding were once a year at the end of the year, which is about what the stock market has done over several extended periods.

Value After Year

	1	5	10	25	40	50
Save $1 Per Day	$365	$2,251	$5,958	$38,709	$185,147	$508,462
Save $2 Per Day	$730	$4,501	$11,917	$77,418	$370,294	$1,016,924
Save $5 Per Day	$1,825	$11,253	$29,792	$193,545	$925,734	$2,542,310

Saving a dollar a day would have grown to more than a half a million dollars after 50 years. Now, to use this plan you have to start young or double up on the amounts in the early years. But even if we start late, as I did, we can enjoy the feeling of financial success and also leave something to our kids when we pass on. However, it is advisable to set up a trust account so your money can't be withdrawn in an untimely manner. The most important point of all is for young people to start saving when they get their first job. If they do this, they will have financial security—something that escapes most people—and I can assure you they won't be in a food line at some point in the future.

Now, back to what I said earlier about the years from 25 to 40. You will note that just by saving $2 per day, you would have $77,418 at the end of 25 years, and a whopping $370,294 after 40 years. This is the "miracle" of compounding. The larger amounts compound so much faster in later years than in the beginning. To be sure, any amount we save will help us stay out of the food lines, but people who are wise enough to start early will have financial security. This idea is simple. As you read it, if you don't know how to go about setting up a stock market investment plan, seek out someone you know and trust to help you. It's still true, ***Your Future Begins Today***.

Other Great SBPRA Books by Jim Davidson

Better Than The Best

If there has ever been a book in today's modern era that deserves and needs to be "in every home" this is it. This book contains the wisdom of the ages and has a plethora of life-changing principles and concepts that will be inspirational and challenging to all who read it. Included are 60 of Jim Davidson's best col-

The Best Columns Selected From Over Thirteen-hundred The Author Has Written

BETTER
THAN THE
BEST

1st

By
Jim Davidson

Noted Author, Public Speaker & Nationally Syndicated Newspaper Columnist & Radio Commentator

umns from over 1,300 he has written, selected by a committee of reviewers.

Some of the titles include: "Welfare and Unwed Mothers," "Don't Let Go of the Rope," "The Greatest Profession of Them All," "A Letter from Prison," "The Obituary for Common Sense," "The Shoji Tabuchi Story," "Who Held Your Ladder,"

"The History of American Legion Baseball" and "A Test for First-Time Parents."

Due to the fact we learn from repetition, to receive the greatest benefit, read a couple of columns each morning as part of your daily devotional. This book will be a terrific gift for Christmas, weddings, birthdays, graduations, and other special occasions. It is available from Amazon, BarnesandNoble.com and other online retailers. For a personalized copy, send $20 (includes postage and handling) to Jim Davidson, 2 Bentley Dr. Conway, AR 72034

The Best of Jim Davidson

The Best of Jim Davidson is a fantastic book. It contains 60 three-minute radio shows that have been broadcast on more than 300 stations coast to coast. Our radio sponsors are furnished transcripts of the shows and listeners can request a copy of the ones that speak to them in a powerful and meaningful

way. Thousands and thousands of listeners did this, and a great number wrote to Jim to commend him on his program and say how much his timely topics have meant to them.

Some of the titles include "Do You Have Class," "Four Marks of an Educated Person," "How to Raise a Crook," "Your Decisions Will Affect Your Family," "The High Cost of Getting Even," "The Silent Patients Speak," "The Fallacy of Liberal Thinking," "Why it Pays to Advertise," and "Should You Go First." Reading a couple of these shows each morning is a great way start your day. It is available from Amazon, BarnesandNoble. com and other online retailers. For a personalized copy, send $20, (includes postage and handling) to Jim Davidson, 2 Bentley Drive, Conway, AR 72034

My Heartfelt Passion:
Saving Our Nation One Child at a Time

Young children reared in low-income, single-parent families who have no books in the home to read, later become high school drop-outs and illiterate adults. If you have a heart for service, you can change this fact for thousands of these unfortunate children by starting a "Bookcase Literacy Project" in your community.

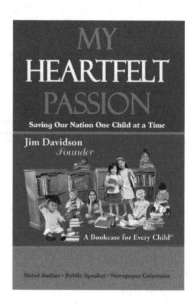

In 2005, this is exactly what the author Jim Davidson did, as he became the Founder of the Conway Bookcase Project. Jim and a committee of his fellow citizens provide 50 personalized bookcases and a starter set of books each year to preschool children enrolled in the local Head Start program.

Since the inception of the project, they have provided 800 bookcases and a starter set of books locally, and more than 2,000 nationwide, as the project has now spread to five other states. After 15 years, Jim has turned the project over to the local Kiwanis Club, where they will likely expand it to every state in the nation. All the details for starting and succeeding with this wonderful project, including a lot of photos, are in the book. You can get a copy from Amazon, BarnesandNoble.com and other online retailers. For a personalized copy signed by the author, send $20, (includes postage and handling) to Jim Davidson, 2 Bentley Drive, Conway, AR 72034.

Choose to Live in Joy

Life goes by in the blink of an eye. It's too short to live upset, angry, resentful or ungrateful. If you look for the good, you'll find it. Choose to be happy, to be at peace. Decide that each day is going to be a great day and grab each moment and make the best of it. Refuse to let negative thoughts take root in your mind and refuse to let negative people and situations drag you down. Trust your journey and know that if you made a mistake, it's okay. See it as a lesson learned and keep moving forward. Spend less time worrying and more time being grateful for those who love you and all of life's goodness. Choose to Live in Joy

Charity M. Richey Bentley

The following blank pages are provided for you to record your future goals and plans, and other thoughts and ideas you wish to review from time to time.

Review Requested:
We'd like to know if you enjoyed the book. Please consider leaving a review on the platform from which you purchased the book.

CPSIA information can be obtained
at www.ICGtesting.com
Printed in the USA
JSHW050843300621
16392JS00002B/5